M.E. PICKLES

Selected Poems

John Heath-Stubbs
SELECTED POEMS

CARCANET

First published in 1990 by
Carcanet Press Limited
208-212 Corn Exchange Buildings
Manchester M4 3BQ

British Library Cataloguing in Publication Data
Heath-Stubbs, John, *1918-*
  Selected Poems
  I. Title
  821'.914

  ISBN 0-85635-900-9

The publisher acknowledges financial assistance from
the Arts Council of Great Britain.

Typeset in 10pt Palatino by Bryan Williamson, Darwen, Lancashire
Printed in England by SRP Ltd., Exeter

Contents

5

7

The Don Juan Triptych

Do you see that old man over there? – He was once a gentleman's
  gentleman;
His skull is bald and wrinkled like a leathery snake's egg;
His forehead is not high, but his eyes, though horny, are cunning,
Like an old jackdaw's beginning to moult a few grey feathers;
His nose is sharp like a weasel's, and his lips always a little smiling,
His narrow shoulders crouched forward, hinting a half-finished
  bow.
Did you notice how beautifully white and smooth and soft his
  hands were?
His coat is dowdy as the dusty shards of a house-haunting beetle,
His cuffs and collar not quite white, like the foam on a fouled
  mill-race.
But Fear flickers over his face – now settling like a fly
On his sunken cheeks, now haunting his blurred eyes;
And his pale mouth is always ready to fall open and gasp and
  shriek . . . .
  Night after night he's here, in all weathers,
Drinking. They say his wife is a shrew and holds her head high
For all that once . . . . Night after night, under the yellow lantern-
  light,
Always the same old chair in the corner, night after night.
  But he likes to talk to a stranger – it makes a nice change.
Why don't you buy him a drink and get him talking?
  He can remember his master well – those were the days! –
Feast days, Carnival days – fans and flowers and bright silk shawls
Tossing like a poppy-patched cornfield the wind dishevels,
And then milky moonlight flowing over close-kept courtyards;
And while his master climbed the balcony, he would keep watch,
Whistle and rub his hands and gaze at the stars –
His co-panders; or there were mandolins murmuring
Lies under windows that winked and slyly slid open;
Or the hand's clutch and half-humorous gasp of the escapade,
And after a doubling hare's turn, choking laughter at fooled
  footsteps
Trotting away down wrong turnings; or when cornered,
The sardonic, simple, decided flash of a sword – his master's
  sword.
And he can remember that night when he stood on the terrace
Sunning himself in black beams of vicarious sin,
While the waltz whispered within;

9

And three unaccountable late-comers came,
And gave no name –
(But she in the blue brocade is Anna:
And she has forged her outraged chastity into a blade
Of thin sharp ice-coloured steel; her hair is brown
And her eyebrows arched and black like two leaping salmon
Seen against the sun-flecked foam of a weir down-rushing;
And like a slim white hound unleashed she snuffs for the blood
Of a father's killer. And not far away is Elvira:
She wears silver and black and is heavily veiled
And has laid a huge jewelled crucifix over her hungry heart
In vain; for she is like an old frosty-feathered gyrfalcon,
With chrysolite eyes, mewed-up now, whose inactive perch
Frets her hooked feet; who cannot bear to gaze out
At the blue sky-paths slashed by young curving wings;
Her heart is a ruined tower from which snake-ivy
Creeps, fit to drag down an oak and smother him in dark green
      leaves.)
But the windows were all golden-spotted with candles,
Shadowed by dancing shapes; till above the silken strings
Flute and violin had trailed across the evening – a cry:
Zerlina, like a wounded hare tangled in that black net.
It is very quiet in the graveyard – a strange place to be waiting
      for him;
The moonlight hints queer perjuries – for all the Dead
Are tucked up snug in mud; we have heaped vast lumps of masonry
Over their heads and their feet, fenced them round with crosses
And stones scrawled over with white lies; we have given them
      flowers
Against the stench, and stopped their nostrils with mud;
We have lighted candles for hollow sockets; they will not trouble us;
They cannot see to climb the slippery stairs of their vault;
They are blind spectators who have long dropped out of the game –
But what if they didn't play fair? What if cold stone
Should speak, and offer unwanted advice? What if quite suddenly
This polished transparently reasonable world were shattered?
When the soft curtain of the night is ripped up by the bray of
      trombones,
And a dumb stone abstraction can speak, and the madman invites
      it to supper –
That is no laughing matter. If you are young and well-born
And have no heart, it seems you can go home and laugh,
Drink wine and do yourself well; but he, Leporello,
A poor man, sir, always attentive to business, no great scholar,

Had never thought of these things, didn't know how to deal with
    the dead gentleman,
Or Hell stretching out a flaming hungry arm
To snatch the ripe fruit of sin from the lighted banqueting hall.

    So that is why he has always a startled look, that old man;
For he feels he is being watched by dead eyes from behind the
    curtains,
And is still expecting a knock at the door, and a stone foot's tramp
    on the stairs.

DON JUAN MUSES
over the dead body of the Commendatore

How beautiful, white and hard, are the teeth of this dead man –
The cold eyes fixed, and about the rigid mouth
The wrinkled lines of pain, like mountain canyons.
I have looked often upon the faces of the Dead,
And seen them carried with naked feet – bodies that once had
    been
Beautiful, obscure and draped in a plain coarse habit,
The stiff impersonal lines of Francis or Dominic –
To the cells of the grave, that always silent college.

And I remember the Day of the Dead; the offerings
Of flowers and fruit, and cakes set at their doors
By the country people, the hooded figures chanting,
And the many lights moving at noon in the sunlit square.

And now in this dark room, in the pause before
The blood is wiped from the blade, before the outcry
Begins, of the servants, and the woman's animal sobbing,
Before the scuffle in the street and the get-away,
I gaze on his cold face, where my own pride's image
Stares back at me – paternal body, stiff,
As though already he were turning to stone –
And so I wonder if this thing was not always
That which I most desired – oh, through the nights,
Those silver nights under a moon of summer,
When I carved my lust into song, or hid my face
In the dark forest of a woman's hair, or sought the comfort
And softness of their flesh; for pain deep-stemmed
Within the marrow, tension of the sinew,
Shall get no final comforting, until

11

I feel my living hand in a stone hand's clasp,
A stone man's eyes reflect my arrogance.

DONNA ELVIRA

That stone death walking the castle corridors,
Whose clanking tread rouses the foxes' bark
Overhead in the high sierra, under a darkened moon,
And sends an echo to these worn battlements; his eyes
Are hollows of the grave, full of blue candles,
Clefts in the mountain's granite, where bright riders,
Black-horsed, with streaming hair, dash to oblivion –
John, it is you he is looking for. He is your fear:
The solitary spectre
Who roars in the labyrinth's centre, in a low vault
Where naked and alone you fight in dreams,
And start from your lover's arms, under a light sheet,
Moaning in sleep, while she lies quiet as a sea
And morning's fingers twitch at the dead curtains.

That striding man in marble I, too, have seen,
Who have known you, as they have never known,
Those others, others: the ladies moving
In Moorish gardens, bright as roses, light as fountains
Falling in laughter between the tamarisk hedges,
Or muffled at Mass with stars behind their veils,
For whom love was a dance on a glass floor,
Tricky, with peacock steps, or posturings
Of the white-tufted crane beside a sunset pool;
Who tripped and fell, poor dolls, their jointed limbs
Snapped in the tangled wires the puppet-master held.
Or the clustered nuns, murmuring like black bees
Home to their stone hive, into whose dreams
You suddenly pranced, hot as a painted devil
Out of their picture-books; or simpering,
With your fake martyr's wounds, your sacred heart upon your
    sleeve,
Peeped from the saints' procession over the altar, soft-mouthed
    and meek
As any anatomical flayed Bartholomew,
Or young Sebastian hedgehogged with arrows.

The peasant girls, gossiping by the fountain,
Or silly as their geese at noon under the cork-trees,

12

Giggle and shrink, seeing your riding shadow
Skim on the pasture, your tall high-stepping horse
Galloping back to the predatory castle
Perched on the crags like a harsh-feathered buzzard.
For them you are legendary as that long-nosed goblin
Who skulks by twilight underneath the eaves,
Or the green-toothed ogre in the Goth-king's grave,
Snoring amongst his gold, who every May-day night
Claims a plump virgin for his supper there.
But I was proud-born of a metalled race,
And as a girl I dreamed a duke or a prince
To be my only husband; or else, perhaps,
Married in a long black veil, to lie alone,
A grove of cedars, where only the white Dove
Might come, and brood, and build his secret nest.
But when I spoke of this, Pasquita, our old nurse,
Combing my long locks by the firelight, would laugh, and say:
"What, these to be shorn away! Lie cold, then, to the cold moon!
No, girl – but these are snares
To catch some wild lover – the bandit-king,
Who will make you rich from his gold-cave in the mountains,
And kidnapped countesses to be your waiting women;
Or the phantom huntsman who rides on windy nights
Over the hills, chasing the ghosts of kings."

But once, in the market-place,
I peered between the curtains of my litter
And saw a gipsy-girl dancing among the crowd;
Flaunting like a flower her brown body, she fixed her eyes –
Eye of a gipsy, eye of a wolf –
Upon the man she wanted, and drew him forward,
Swaying her hips and arms, and her young breasts,
To the rhythm of castanets and clapping hands;
She seemed as ancient
As a goddess painted on a cave's flat wall
In red and yellow ochre; and beckoned him –
A tall young mule-driver – to love as to destruction.
Then my blood cried that I was one with her,
And one with the shifting moon, and the harsh sea,
And the hungry grave, the last of all your lovers.

You have pulled down my pride. There is none left;
And my dreams shrivel like rose-leaves in the fire.
I have run bare-foot up and down the streets

Like any raddled whore who's lost her swaggerer.
Your servant, too, has led me by the snout:
That little man, with a weasel's nose,
Who scans the dry anatomy of your desires,
And has cast-up, and ruled in his account-book
The profit and the loss of all your lust.
He knows you, too; therefore he, too,
Shall meet that stone death on the stairs, and live.

But now I am the black-faced moon that speaks to your ebb-tide;
The Banshee, with a night-bird's voice,
Trailing my veils of shade, boding of death.
Be free then from my love, whose whimpering muzzle
Follows your heel no more. Another hand
Arrests your fingers on the passionate sword-hilt.
At last you have been caught; put a bold face on it –
A dirty schoolboy breaking bounds at night –
But I was the night, and I the apple-tree.
How transient you are –
Poor lord, poor lover, less than a ghost,
Who have no flesh and blood but our desire.

Tschaikowskian Poem

And as we came down by the staircase –
Broad the balustrade, shining and bronze in the lustre
Of hanging lights, smooth and strong to the touch like your arm –
Down the grand sweep of the staircase eagerly stepping,
We two, to the lighted ballroom, the swirl of my music,
You paused and said: "The moon is a strange questing
Creature embodied out over these wide white plains;
But whether hunter or huntress, I do not know –
But whether hunter or hunted!"
And your mouth smiled, though while your eyes were thoughtful.
I said: "She is a maiden pursuing, or a wild white falcon
Unmewed through the skies, or she is a hind, or a hound,
Or a frightened hare – the bewitched princess who wanders
There through the snow-covered night and over the pine-trees,
Or a wild swan perhaps, or a wizened dwarf,
Back-crook'd and broken because of his burden of silver,
Who stumbles home in the cold to his cave in the mountains!

14

But let us go down now to the lighted ballroom
Where they are expecting us, for the dance begins."
And we went down into the hall, alone no longer.

   And standing by a window a girl said:
"Only once I saw one, once, once;
Far out over the snow, in a hard winter –
When I was a little girl, at our country place.
And Anya, our old nurse, said: 'Look, child –
Come to the window, and I will show you a wolf.'
(For often the long evenings she had told us of them)
And there it went, the lonely one, like a great dog –
But hindquarters narrow and drooping, like a cowardly dog –
Hungry nose to the snow, onward, onward.
But sometimes it paused, and scraped in its tracks, and raised
Its great head to the bitter skies, and howled."

   Oh curved, curved in a scroll the violin's neck and carved
With concentration of the patient hand;
And tight those strings and quick to break in the harsh
Air, and in the inclement weather;
And shrill, shrill the song of the strings, when the horse-hair
     sweeps
Caressingly upon them. And the flutes ice-blue, and the harps
Like melting frost, and the trumpet marching, marching
Like fire above them, like fire through the frozen pine-trees.
And the dancers came, swirling, swirling past me –
Plume and swansdown waving, white plume over the gold hair,
Arms held gallantly, and silk-talking – and an eye caught
In the candle-shadow, and the curve of a mouth
Going home to my heart (the folly of it!), going home to my heart!

   And the black-browed girl by the window said, remembering:
"Always in my dreams it is thus, always in my dreams –
Snow and moonlight, snow and the dark pines moaning,
Fur over my body, and my feet small,
Delicate and swift to run through the powdery snow;
And my sharp mouth to the ground, hungry, hungry,
And always onward, onward, alone, alone...."

   Moon, moon, cold mouth over the pine-trees,
Or are you hunting me, or I pursuing?

An Heroic Epistle

from William Congreve to Anne Bracegirdle
circa 1729

Now it has all gone black, you are more than ever
The cadence of a voice to me, the turn of a prose phrase;
For my words in your mouth were a movement in time,
Like your hand's movement suddenly spreading the white
Fan, your turned wrist twisting the air;
Or the curve of your white neck, caught in a slant-light,
The tilt of your chin, and your smile mocking, mocking –
And then your laughter – and so your voice again.
    And never, my dear, was proud man's tenderness
Like this, never such patience;
A love not like a boy's love, nor a man loving like a boy, but rather
As one who has perfected some instrument
Of calculation – crystal, and chased gold,
And swinging steel, and mirrors set aslant
To each refraction of the sun's bright rays –
As such a man, long days in a dark workshop,
Brings forth this cold child of his quiet brain,
And after with delight knows all its rhythms,
The moods of its clear bright body –
Such was my love for you – the poet
Breathing his words into your silver throat,
Knowing each grace of your tongue, each turn of your hand,
Your musical body, so much more apt to movement,
Thus and thus, than mine, a man's, hard-thewed –
Yes, even the bright mysteries of your woman's body,
More than mere lover dares know – in the clear hard brain.
    But that was many years ago, in another century,
When love was still a ladder, and the brain,
The burning wit, crowned all the body's dancing.
Then was it thought crossing thought as the hand the hand –
At the point of contact, pleasure, at the intersection
Of wits, the laughter....
    And at the turn of time our music reached
Its fulness, as a conceived child,
Closed in the female body, knows its time –
That play was my crown of myrtle, fillet of laughter,
My gift to you, and yours to me, and ours to the world –
And spurned by the world; but I have done with the world.
    And also in that year
John Dryden died, that great builder in words,

16

Poor and dislaurelled. They say that at his burying
Were strange things done; and it were something meet
That old man's corpse was carried off with laughter
Of fools, intoxication
(Which in the ancient times was of the gods)
Though only of fools.
   And so that age passed with him.
And now we live in a rounded time, rounded
With a low horizon of feeling until men break it.
We have forgotten the old high modes of loving,
And the song's poise is gone.
The intellect squats twisted like a spider,
A tortured, hunch-backed poet; or lurks, exiled,
Westward, within a starved and savage country –
(He will die mad.) There is the Duchess too,
Who will have an ivory image made when I am gone,
To sit at her table, smile, and nod its head –
But the laughter is gone, and youth is gone, and you
Are gone to pray.
You cannot make of me a saint, nor I
Of you a sinner – but the pride of wit
Is whittled down, and our long battle now
Lacks auditors, lacks point.
The fire is gone – we may find tenderness,
From each to each, uncomplicate, at last –
An actress who has left the Stage behind,
An old blind gentleman who once wrote plays.

For the Nativity

Shepherds, I sing you, this winter's night
Our Hope new-planted, the womb'd, the buried Seed:
For a strange Star has fallen, to blossom from a tomb,
And infinite Godhead circumscribed, hangs helpless at the breast.

Now the cold airs are musical, and all the ways of the sky
Vivid with moving fires, above the hills where tread
The feet – how beautiful! – of them that publish peace.

The sacrifice, which is not made for them,
The angels comprehend, and bend to earth

17

Their worshipping way. Material kind Earth
Gives Him a Mother's breast, and needful food.

A Love, shepherds, most poor,
And yet most royal, kings,
Begins this winter's night;
But oh, cast forth, and with no proper place,
Out in the cold He lies!

The Divided Ways

in memory of Sidney Keyes

He has gone down into the dark cellar
To talk with the bright-faced Spirit with silver hair;
But I shall never know what word was spoken there.

My friend is out of earshot. Our ways divided
Before we even knew we had missed each other.
For he advanced
Into a stony wilderness of the heart,
Under a hostile and a red-clawed sun;
All that dry day, until the darkness fell,
I heard him going, and shouting among the canyons.
But I, struck backward from the eastern gate,
Had turned aside, obscure,
Beneath the unfriendly silence of the moon,
My long white fingers on a small carved lute.
There was a forest, and faces known in childhood
Rose unexpected from the mirrored pools;
The trees had hands to clutch my velvet shoulders,
And birds of fever sang among the branches;
Till the dark vine-boughs, breaking as I seized them,
And dripping blood, cried out with my own voice:
"I also have known thirst, and the wanderer's terror!..."

But I had lost my friend and the mountain paths;
And if there might have been another meeting –
The new sun rising in a different sky,
Having repaired his light in the streams of Ocean,
And the moon, white and maternal, going down
Over the virgin hills – it is too late
Ever to find it now.

And though it was in May that the reptile guns
And breeze-fly bullets took my friend away,
It is no time to forge a delicate idyll
Of the young shepherd, stricken, prone among
The flowers of spring, heavy with morning dew,
And emblematic blood of dying gods;
Or that head pillowed on a wave's white fleece,
Softly drowning in a Celtic sea.
This was more harsh and meaningless than winter.

But now, at last, I dare avow my terror
Of the pale vampire by the cooling grate;
The enemy face that doubled every loved one;
My secret fear of him and his cold heroes;
The meaning of the dream
Which was so fraught with trouble for us both;
And how, through this long autumn
(Sick and tempestuous with another sorrow)
His spirit, vexed, fluttered among my thoughts,
A bird returning to the darkened window –
The hard-eyed albatross with scissor bill.
And I would ask his pardon for this weakness.

But he is gone where no hallooing voice
Nor beckoning hand can ever call him back;
And what is ours of him
Must speak impartially for all the world;
There is no personal word remains for me,
And I pretend to find no meaning here.
Though I might guess that other Singer's wisdom
Who saw in Death a dark immaculate flower,
And tenderness in every falling autumn,
This abstract music will not bring again
My friend to his warm room:
Inscrutable the darkness covers him.

Hart Crane

The green-wombed sea proves now a harsher lover
And more acquisitive than her easy sons,
As furtively the crab, her agent, scans
The inventory of heart and brain and liver;

19

You suffer here, beyond the plunge of diver,
Her deeper perfidies: the warm stream runs
With gifts of boughs and birds, dead Indians
To each fresh voyager; yet still, deceiver,

Her laced white fingers lap a hollow land,
Where with false rhetoric through the hard sky
The bridges leap, twanged by dry-throated wind,

And crowded thick below, with idiot eye
The leaning deadmen strive to pierce the dim
Tunnels and vaults, which agate lamps illume.

Ibycus

When the city cast out the best
   In a clamour of indecision,
I had no words to waste
   Cobbling up their division;
I unhooked the lyre from its peg,
   Turned ship to the Samian shore.
I call no man to witness
   But the clanging birds of the air.

The quince-tree garden is shattered,
   The vine-shoots fail in Spring;
Down from the Thracian mountains,
   On fire with the lightning,
Love comes, like a blackguard wind.
   Love was betrayal and fear.
I call no man to witness
   But the clanging birds of the air.

The open-handed I praise,
   Great-souled Polycrates,
Pride of whose tinted galleons
   Ruled the Ionian seas.
Treachery took him – nailed
   For the crows to peck him bare.
I call no man to witness
   But the clanging birds of the air.

20

Twilight: a narrow place:
    Armed men blocking the road.
Gold glisters on my finger.
    In chevron high overhead
The southward-journeying cranes –
    What Erinnyes are here?
I call no man to witness
    But the clanging birds of the air.

Address not Known

So you are gone, and are proved bad change, as we had always
    known,
And I am left lonely in London the metropolitan city,
Perhaps to twist this incident into a durable poem –
The lesson of those who give their love to phenomenal beauty.

I am coming to think now that all I have loved were shadows
Strayed up from a dead world, through a gap in a raped tomb,
Or where the narcissus battens in mythological meadows:
Your face was painted upon the coffin-lid from Fayoum.

Is this my pain that is speaking? The pain was not long protracted:
I make a statement, forgive the betrayal, the meanness, the theft.
Human, I cannot suppose you had planned all that was enacted:
Fortitude must be procured to encounter the hollowness left.

The sun will not haver in its course for the lack of you,
Nor the flowers fail in colour, nor the bird stint in its song.
Only the heart that wanted somehow to have opened up
Finds the frost in the day's air, and the nights which appear too long

Shepherd's Bush Eclogue

As I walked to Shepherd's Bush, I perceived it was truly pastoral,
For May, a Monna Vanna, a Mopsa, had tossed her cumuli,
Her flocks of white wool, into the azure and virginal
Fields of pure air that all over London lie.

I breathed a *Sursum Corda*; but a grief-worm in my breast
Twisted, and told me how all the riches of Spring
Are only a sandy fistful that runs through our fingers to waste;
For each of us is into continual exile travelling –

Moving away from life, and love, and lovers, and the light,
Since we fell from the primal garden into this troubled stream.
Not here, not here is our franchise: these images of delight
Still fail and fleet and cheat us in the context of a dream.

O Muse, I said then, dear sister, how long will your voice be mute?
This is your season, surely: these moments furnish your cue –
Praise this delicious weather with your accentor's throat;
In the heart of a poem's crystal alone can the Spring come true.

Churchyard of Saint Mary Magdalene, Old Milton

Here, where my father lies under the ornamental plum,
Geese step in the next farm-field, while to the Rectory elms
The rooks fly home. *Dominus exaltatio mea* –
The eagle rising with its sprig of acorns.

Feet deep in sticky clay, under the kempt grasses,
Under the anglo-saxon, and the celtic crosses,
The Indian judges lie, the admirals, the solicitors,
The eccentric ladies, and the shopkeepers,
The unenterprising who would not go to the town,
The charwoman with a cleft palate, the jobbing gardener,
And the four Germans who fell, some few years back,
Out of a sky of trouble, smashed
In an empty field – these have
Their regulation crosses too, of wood,
And scattered flowers, left by the prisoners:
The old woman whom I meet
Remarks that after all they were somebody's sons
And we would do as much for our people.

"The writer returns to the scene of his childhood" –
Where he loitered and looked at the rooks and the geese and the
        turkeys,
Or sought for wild barley by the churchyard gate –

22

Elegiac Stanzas

in memory of William Bell

Fretful, with all her fine deceits of mind
About her still, and still unchanged, the city
Opens her grey heart to mild January,
With medlars and mortality in her hand;

Where in their windy towers the old men weep,
Remembering how soon the goddess fled
(Before they woke and found how youth was dead)
While she but touched their parted lips in sleep.

But I recall that Irish sorcerer –
His table set, the tall glasses of wine,
All Souls' tide summoning at the bell's last groan
His wandering shades to a thin-fumed banquet here –

Whose lonely ceremony I need not prove,
Since pausing at the end of every street,
Rustling homewards through these skies I greet
Poems, like birds, that seek the sacred grove.

But when the night is come, from their sublime
And baroque heavens the great musicians bend:
Sebastian Bach, eternity on his mind,
And Monteverdi, between the seraphim,

Yet whispering now with the year's gentlest breath –
"*Zefiro torna, torna...*" – whose complaint
Is formal landscapes and the nymph's lament,
And how Spring brought no solace for her grief.

Oxford, January 21st – 23rd, 1949

Care in Heaven

How many times they do come (if you will receive it),
So gay, with a light hand, and a brisk pinion
Cutting the blue air, that stands above London, even –
So, in a phrase of song,

In a half-hour's peace, lying like a moment of love
Upon our wounds, affect us;
Telling we are only a footstep from the garden,
From the golden world, from the shoemakers' holiday –
How near we were to finding our lost childhood.

So courteous they are. Then why should we refuse them
If to-morrow they come back in their formal livery,
Their panoply of humiliation, to pummel
With fiery sword-hilts upon the heart's closed doors?
These are dark nuncios; they have the king's commission.

Let it be Michaelmas: the failing of the leaf,
The time of the blue daisy – when the chief of the heavenly birds
Strikes at the glistering snake, who falls
Like a wreath, like a wraith of smoke, among
Those hemlock-umbels, the autumn constellations.

Bird-Song in New England

Jargon of cat-bird, purple finch, or song-sparrow –
Your notes now breathe a life
To stiff Victorian woodcuts, known in boyhood,
From yellowing books of Natural History, *Tableaux
Of Animated Nature*. The chimney-swift
Goes splitter-splutter into the twilight, different
From my shrill subfusc devil-screamer, whirling
Up through Lord Nuffield's smoke-smeared Oxford sky
To doze till dawn, the footless one, his cradle
The lullabying currents of warm air.

The myths retire,
Shyly, to their museums; or here they dwindle
Into a summer haze of Tanglewood tales
Twice-told to children by a nervous student.
For if the emigrant Muse
Forsook Cephissus, Arno, or her Thames,
By Charles's banks to plant her candid footprints,
It was occasional; conceded, Indian ghosts,
Reproachful, haunt these parklands and this outcrop.

And at a bird's cry, should one say:
"Some hapless nymph of chaste Diana's train,
Pursued by hirsute Pan, in her extremity
Besought the prudish goddess – 'Aid me, do,
Sweet Phoebe, Phoebe!' – whereat the Delian
Alert in her Olympian mansions heard,
Descended (in machine) and – Ovid mark! –
Transmogrified the virgin to a bird"?

Those syllables relate
Only a whistling, melancholy call.

State of Massachusetts
July 1955

Canso

When spring airs fondle
And the nightingale
In the olivaster
  Harbours and sings,
And the moon's candle
Numinous and pale
Hangs high to foster
  Increase of things –

My heart discourses
Contrariwise:
How beauty is fallible
  In all her pride;
The season passes;
Embrowns the rose;
Nothing perdurable,
  Things faint and fade.

Thus our mortality
Fortune derides;
For love's mutations
  We learn to weep;
And no sodality
But it corrodes
Through time's collusions,
  Darkness, and sleep.

So we, being homeless
When spring rides high,
Should make obeisance
    In her cool vault
To the grave goddess
Of the moonless sky,
That her beneficence
    Go not by default.

It is convenient
We take this guise
To hold her revered;
    That in all terms,
She may be lenient,
And we, likewise,
Not unprepared
    When winter comes

Les Saintes-Maries-de-la-Mer
April 1953

The Lady's Complaint

I speak of that lady I heard last night,
    Maudlin over her gin and water,
In a sloppy bar with a fulvous light
    And an air that was smeared with smoke and laughter:
    How youth decamps and cold age comes after,
In fifty years she had found it true –
    She sighed for the damage that time had brought her:
"Oh, after death there's a judgement due.

"What once was as sleek as a seal's pelt,
    My shapeless body has fallen from grace;
My soul and my shoes are worn down to the welt,
    And no cosmetic can mask my face,
    As under talcum and oxide you trace
How the bones stick out, and the ghost peeps through –
    A wanderer, I, in Wraith-bone Place,
And after death there's a judgement due.

28

"My roundabout horses have cantered away,
    The gilded and garrulous seasons are flown;
What echo is left of the rag-time bray
    Of the tenor sax and the sousaphone?
    But I was frightened to sleep alone
(As now I must do, as now I must do)
    And a chittering bat-voice pipes 'Atone,
For after death there's a judgement due.'

"Green apples I bit when I was green,
    My teeth are on edge at the maggoty core;
Life is inclement, obscure, obscene;
    Nothing's amusing – not any more;
    But love's abrasions have left me sore –
To hairy Harry and half-mast Hugh
    I gave the love I was starving for,
And after death there's a judgement due.

"Potentate, swirling in stark cold air
    The corn from the husks – I offer to you
My terror-struck and incredulous prayer,
    For after death there's a judgement due."

Girl with Marionettes

(Leeds City Varieties)
to John Betjeman

They hold their own, not the wire-puller's laws,
As each its wicked, sensual life assumes;
The prancing skeleton gained our applause.

That invocation gave our laughter pause:
These manikins our merriment exhumes –
They hold their own, not the wire-puller's laws.

The grave-faced girl, thus, cautiously withdraws
Them from their box, like mummies from old tombs –
The prancing skeleton gained our applause.

The erotic nautch-doll, draped in tinselled gauze,
Twitches her stiff limbs to Ketélby's neumes;
They hold their own, not the wire-puller's laws.

29

And vanishing at last, as with no cause –
Magnesium flash, and puff of bluish fumes –
The prancing skeleton gained our applause.

To abolish chaos, and restore guffaws,
Three teddy-bears in hand, she now presumes;
They hold their own, not the wire-puller's laws,
The prancing skeleton gained our applause.

Epitaph for Thaïs

Traveller, under this stone lies all that remains – of our sister,
    Arete, servant of Christ; alkaline sands of Natroun
Hold here a wonder, those limbs which once lent their contours
    to Thaïs
    (God has forgiven her sins – scarlet, now whiter than snow).
Ask not how many young men their fortunes let slip, and careers,
    Chancing one night on her couch (and it was worth it, they said);
Neo-Platonic sages failed to show up at their lectures –
    Dream of the touch of her lips, metaphysics go hang!
Praising one of her nipples, there was a poet composed an
    Epic in twenty-two books (no one peruses it now).
Alexandria's side-streets are always full of such rumours
    (Keep to the lives of the Saints, these are the gossip of Heaven).
All is altered now; she who was bound to the shameless
    Demon the heathen revere, Aphrodite the Rose,
Now is made free of the golden-causewayed city of Zion
    (Love that accomplishes all, glory be given to Thee).
Athanäel our brother with his rough rhetoric tamed this
    Lamb that so widely had strayed, coaxing it back to the fold.

Athanäel has left us; dying, they say in despair – he
    Could find no quiet nor rest, such are the snares of the Fiend –
So distracted his prayers the rose-tinctured body of Thaïs,
    Satan into his den clawed that apostatized soul.

Did you suppose, O you who pass by, this hetaira
    Yielded herself to a god, not exacting her price?
What more costly a gem could Heaven itself afford than,
    Dear-bought and bright, a soul predestined, to her fee?

30

The Cave of the Nymphs

Hushed, haunted the cave – a gathering point
For time and eternity. One entrance
For men, subject to death,
One, open to the sky,
For the Undying. In this place,
Where the quiet nymphs weave purple cloth,
And hive the learnèd bees – archetypes,
Images, symbols.

But Ulysses,
Ulysses of the many stratagems,
Was unaware of this. He shook himself (grandson
of Autolycus, the wolf-man) suddenly awake
Like a great canine. He rubbed the salt from his eyes,
Dismissing the images of night and journeying:
The snatching horror, the sucking whirlpool,
Canticle of the death-birds,
Possessive and beast-attended
Goddesses, the geometrical gardens.
He knew where he was. The landscape
Was not the deceptive pastoral simplicity
Of the cannibals' island, and not
The hothouse vegetation of Lotos-land,
Nor spruce and silver-birch
Of the Laestrygones' fjord. It was limestone;
It was tamarisks; it was olives
And vine-stocks gnawed by goats.
It was Ithaca at last. And was dangerous.
Therefore, out in the sunlight,
Meeting a shepherd-boy,
He started once more to lie –
It was almost routine with him now –
Improvising a cover-story. But with so much blague,
And such a ready tongue,
He began to enjoy it. And that other,
Knowing it would all come out,
Could not refrain from revealing herself –
The goddess who was on his side –
And chaffed him too. So they stood there,
The man and the Immortal, like a pair of friends
Who understood each other
Too well to talk much.

31

And as he turned to go,
She still smiled after him. But if
The perdurable and inviolate heart
Of immortal Wisdom might grieve, it ached then
For what it could never know:
For not to know death is to know nothing
Of the wonder of deliverance; and to be free
Of the wide aether, and the white peaks of Olympos,
And all the bounds of the world and the backward-flowing Ocean,
Is never to know and love
One patch of earth as home.

                    But Ulysses,
Ulysses who had made a good journey,
Was unaware of this. He had gone to look for
A wife he had not met
For twenty years, and a son
Who must now be a stranger to him.
For he had come home;
Which is the whole point of the story.

Not Being Oedipus

Not being Oedipus he did not question the Sphinx
Nor allow it to question him. He thought it expedient
To make friends and try to influence it.
In this he entirely succeeded,

And continued his journey to Thebes. The abominable thing
Now tame as a kitten (though he was not unaware
That its destructive claws were merely sheathed)
Lolloped along beside him –

To the consternation of the Reception Committee.
It posed a nice problem: he had certainly overcome
But not destroyed the creature – was he or was he not
Entitled to the hand of the Princess

Dowager Jocasta? Not being Oedipus
He saw it as a problem too. For frankly he was not
By natural instinct at all attracted to her.
The question was soon solved –

Solved itself, you might say; for while they argued
The hungry Sphinx, which had not been fed all day,
Sneaked off unobserved, penetrated the royal apartments,
And softly consumed the lady.

So he ascended the important throne of Cadmus,
Beginning a distinguished and uneventful reign.
Celibate, he had nothing to fear from ambitious sons;
Although he was lonely at nights,

With only the Sphinx, curled up upon his eiderdown.
Its body exuded a sort of unearthly warmth
(Though in fact cold-blooded) but its capacity
For affection was strictly limited.

Granted, after his death it was inconsolable,
And froze into its own stone effigy
Upon his tomb. But this was self-love, really –
It felt it had failed in its mission.

While Thebes, by common consent of the people, adopted
His extremely liberal and reasonable constitution,
Which should have enshrined his name – but not being Oedipus,
It vanished from history, as from legend.

Plato and the Waters of the Flood

In one of the remoter parts of Asia Minor, near what was once the southern
boundary of the Phrygians, there is a warm spring flanked by a Hittite monument,
and known to the Turks as Plato's Spring. The reason for the name is that it was
at this spot, according to Arab legend, that Plato succeeded in stopping the Flood
by making the waters run underground.

W.K.C. GUTHRIE, *Orpheus and Greek Religion*

When on Armenian Ararat
    Or Parnassus ridge
Scrunched the overloaded keel,
    Pelican, ostrich,
Toad, rabbit, and pangolin –
    All the beasts of the field –
Scrambled out to possess once more
    Their cleansed and desolate world.

33

Plato, by that fountain,
    Spoke to the swirling deep:
"Retire, you waters of Chaos,
    Flow retrograde, and sleep;
Above the swift revolving heavens
    Rule the intelligible,
Chaste and undecaying ideas;
    Brackish waters, fall!"

Plato, in the academic grove,
    Among the nightingales,
Expounded to wide-eyed ephebes
    His geometric rules;
Reared a republic in the mind
    Where only noble lies
Reign; he expelled the poets
    (With courtesy, with praise).

Loaded with useless garlands,
    Down to that fountain
The exiled poets proceeded:
    "When will you rise again,
Ten-horned, seven-headed seraphim,
    Out of your abyss,
Against the beautiful Republic –
    Nor tamed by Plato's kiss?"

Titus and Berenice

"Turn to me in the darkness,
    Asia with your cool
Gardens beyond the desert,
    Your clear, frog-haunted pool;
I seek your reassurance –
    Forget, as I would forget,
Your holy city cast down, the Temple
    That still I desecrate."
"Buzz!" said the blue-fly in his head.

"In darkness master me,
    Rome with your seven hills,

Roads, rhetorical aqueducts,
　　And ravaging eagles;
Worlds are at bitter odds, yet we
　　Can find our love at least –
Not expedient to the Senate,
　　Abominable to the priest."
"Buzz!" said the blue-fly in his head.

Titus the clement Emperor
　　And she, of Herod's house,
Slobbered and clawed each other
　　Like creatures of the stews;
Lay together, then lay apart
　　And knew they had not subdued –
She the insect in his brain,
　　Nor he her angry God.

Note: According to a Jewish tradition Titus was afflicted with an insect in his brain as a punishment for his destruction of the Temple.

Ars Poetica

1

One thing *imprimis* I would have you remember:
Your poetry is no good
Unless it move the heart. And the human heart,
The heart which you must move,
Is corrupt, depraved, and desperately wicked.

Milton denoted poetry
"Simple, sensuous and passionate".
But who has said, my dear,
Human sensuality and human passion
Were ever simple matters?

But poetry is not "emotional truth".
The emotions have much less to do with the business
Than is commonly supposed. No more than the intellect.
The intellect shapes, the emotions feed the poem,
Whose roots are in the senses, whose flower is imagination.

Call it then: "A humane science"
(Like all science concerned
With a world that really exists) – but humane:
Beatrice could request, not command Virgil –
She among the blessed, and he in Limbo –
He can take you as far as the Earthly Paradise
But no further than that.

In Limbo also is the Master of them that know:
But he is a Master. Therefore respect critics,
Especially the uncomfortable ones.

But there is no field of any activity
In which the parable of the wheat and the tares
Is more applicable.

The poem does not propound
Yours or anyone else's opinions,
However admirable, however fascinating;
With luck it may touch the skirts
Of universal Wisdom.

And much the same goes for the passions:
The oaf in love *may* be a poet
Or bumpkin tongue-tied still;
A poet in love may be no less oafish.
And so in eloquence remember
All things exist in Love.

I mentioned just now luck – our Lady Fortune
("Bright-haired daughter of Chaos" I once called her)
She also is an exalted goddess,
Germane to the Muse. Therefore revere her.

2

A poem is built out of words;
And words are not your property.
They are common counters, involved
In private chaffering, and international transactions;
They have been tossed into the caps of beggars, and plonked
On the reception-desks of brothels.

In your case they are the English language:
Not the Greek flute, nor the Roman trumpet,
Nor the Welsh harp, nor the Spanish guitar,
Nor the French clavecin,
But a sound bourgeois piano
Capable of something of each.

You have got to make language say
What it has not said before;
Otherwise why bother – after a millennium,
(And a bit more) of English poetry – and you a wren
Rising from the eagle's back?
Work against language. It is your enemy.
Engage in a bout with it.
But like a Japanese wrestler
You will overcome by not resisting.

3

The words come to you from the commercial districts:
From the shop-bench, and from working in the fields;
But contrary to much of the practice of the age
There is something to be said for politely requesting them
To wipe the mud off their boots
Before they tread on your carpet
(Supposing you own one).

And if they should emerge from the reading-room
Tactfully suggest they remove the cheese-parings,
Dead flies and biscuit-crumbs from among their whiskers.

I have no personal objection
If you want to put on singing robes:
At a ritual you don't wear work-a-day clothes.
But the surplice and chasuble, or the Geneva gown
Are nothing more than the Sunday best
Of a Byzantine gentleman, or a Renaissance scholar;
And any clergyman, I suppose, would look pretty silly
If he walked down the street in them.

So under existing social conditions
You had better think over this matter of your costume
With a certain perspicacity.

A poem is like an iceberg:
Seven-tenths under water
(And what is below the surface –
This may at first have seemed –
To you the most important.)
Like an iceberg – cold, hard,
Jagged and chaste, glittering
With prismatic colours, as it drifts
On unpredictable deep-sea tides. Against it also
The titanic folly of the age
May shatter itself as it goes through its joyless night.

5

"Patience and perseverance
Made a bishop in his reverence."
The proverb ought to have added
"And the charisma of the Holy Ghost."

Mutatis mutandis
(And it is very much *mutandis*)
This likewise is relevant.

So through patience, perseverance, luck and that sort of thing
(I can only wish you luck)
You may arrive at an actual poem –
An interjected remark
At a party which has been going on
For quite a time (and will, we trust, continue);
A party at which you are not
A specially favoured guest
And which you will have to leave before it is over.

Let us hope the others will occasionally recall it.

But to you it will seem a little world.
You will look at your creation and see that it is good.
In this you will be mistaken:
You are not, after all, God.

Lament for the "Old Swan", Notting Hill Gate

The Old Swan has gone. They have widened the road.
A year ago they closed her, and she stood,
The neighbouring houses pulled down, suddenly revealed
In all her touching pretentiousness
Of turret and Gothic pinnacle, like
A stupid and ugly old woman
Unexpectedly struck to dignity by bereavement.

And now she has vanished. The gap elicits
A guarded sentiment. Enough bad poets
Have romanticized beer and pubs,
And those for whom the gimcrack enchantments
Of engraved glass, mahogany, plants in pots,
Were all laid out to please, were fugitives, doubtless,
Nightly self-immersed in a fake splendour.

Yet a Public House perhaps makes manifest also
The hidden City; implies its laws
Of tolerance, hierarchy, exchange.
Friends I remember there, enemies, acquaintances,
Some drabs and drunks, some bores and boors, and many
Indifferent and decent people. They will drink elsewhere.
Anonymous, it harboured
The dreadful, innocent martyrs
Of megalopolis – Christie or Heath.

Now that's finished with. And all the wide
And sober roads of the world walk sensibly onwards
Into the featureless future. But the white swans
That dipped and swam in each great lucid mirror
Remain in the mind only, remain as a lost symbol.

Variation on a Theme by George Darley

It is not beauty I desire
    And not – but not – the virtuous mind:
Marks of potential tragedy –
    These stigmatize the human kind.

39

And lonely in the darkness, I
   Surmise your pain, your loneliness,
And stretch uneasy arms towards
   That inarticulate distress.

If sons and daughters of the gods
   Stride careless through the market-place
What can we but avert our eyes –
   Acknowledge, not demand, their grace?

Although the smooth olympian brow
   Bids Greece and Ilium beware,
More turbid tides on love's dark sea
   Involve us with the siren's hair.

Each hard-faced doctor who expounds
   Within the rigid schools avers
That God Himself loves His elect
   Yet for no merit that is theirs.

And, fuel to the appalling creed,
   By human analogues we know
We do not love the beautiful
   But, loved, they are imputed so.

The Timeless Nightingale

A nightingale sat perched upon
   The trellis of a Samian vine
Beneath whose shade Anacreon
   Strung his slight lyre, and drank his wine;
Far in the Asian highlands then
   The corpse of great Polycrates
Was scorched by sun and stripped by rain,
   Stretched on the cross-bars of two trees;
But the nightingale's lament
   Was for dismembered Itylus:
White-haired Anacreon vainly schemed –
   How could he move Cleobulus.
   The poet took another glass.

Li Po drank his rice-spirit warm:
    Disgraced at court, he sipped alone –
No-one to talk to or make love –
    Himself, his shadow, and the moon;
Above his head, migrating cranes:
    In the wild gorges monkeys howl:
Red-haired, green-eyed barbarians
    Along the utmost marches prowl;
The nightingale (or what bird else
    Chinese convention had assigned)
Fluted of jewelled gardens where
    Drunken immortals ride the wind.
        The poet took another glass.

Upon a greenish sky at dawn
    The sickle of the moon grew dim:
Hafiz still sat there on the lawn:
    A moon-browed Saki poured for him;
Advanced across the Northern hills
    Timur and his crude Turkish band,
To build their pyramids of skulls,
    And fetch the wine to Samarkand;
But the timeless nightingale
    Enamoured of the eternal rose
Cried "Love's in the dark of the candle-flame,
    And nothing quite what we suppose!"
        The poet took another glass.

The true, the blushful Hippocrene
    Was fairish claret, if you please:
Love a bacillus in his lung,
    John Keats was on those perilous seas;
Into the mills of Yorkshire now
    The Luddite gangs walked stark and grim:
The bourgeois Muse was mousy-haired
    And did not only dance with him;
The nightingale inside his head
    Sang on (at once to him and Ruth)
"You're better off when you are dead –
    Truth's Beauty then, and Beauty truth."
        The poet took another, took another glass.

Mozart and Salieri

Salieri encountered Mozart;
  Took him friendly by the arm,
And smiled a thin-lipped ambiguous smile.
  This was Italian charm.

Mozart observed the smile of Salieri
  But was not enough observant,
(For the Angel of Death had called already
  In the guise of an upper servant).

"Maestro," said Salieri "Dear Maestro,
  It is happy that we met."
"We'll end this sharp boy's tricks," he thought
  "He'll not get by – not yet!")

"And as for that post of kapellmeister
  We'll do what we can do."
But something black within him whispered:
  "He is greater, is greater than you.

"He is great enough to oust you, one day,
  And take your place at Court."
("Not if Salieri is Salieri,"
  Salieri thought.)

"It is happy that we met," said Salieri
  "I wish I could ask you to dine –
But I have, alas, a pressing engagement.
  You will stay for a glass of wine?"

No one carried Mozart to nobody's grave
  And the skies were glazed and dim
With a spatter of out-of-season rain
  (Or the tears of the Seraphim).

Then two stern angels stood by that grave
  Saying: "Infidel, Freemason,
We are taking your soul where it willed to be judged
  At the throne of Ultimate Reason."

But the Queen of the Night in coloratura
    Horrors trilled at the sun,
For she looked at the soul of Wolfgang Amadeus
    And she knew she had not won.

They lifted that soul where the great musicians
    In contrapuntal fires
Through unlimited heavens of order and energy
    Augment the supernal choirs.

And the spirit of Johann Sebastian, harrowed
    With abstract darts of love,
Escorted the terrible child Mozart
    Through courteous mansions above.

And hundred-fisted Handel erected
    Great baroque arches of song
As the Cherubim and the Seraphim
    Bandied Mozart along.

But Mozart looked back again in compassion
    Below the vault of the stars
To where the body of Beethoven battered
    Its soul on the prison bars.

Successful Salieri lay dying –
    But now his reason was gone –
In a chamber well-fitted with Louis Seize furniture,
    But dying, dying alone.

Then two small devils, like surpliced choirboys,
    Like salamanders in black and red,
Extracted themselves from the fluttering firelight
    And stood beside the bed.

And they sang to him then in two-part harmony,
    With their little, eunuchoid voices:
"You have a pressing engagement, Salieri,
    In the place of no more choices."

So they hauled down his soul and put it away
    In a little cushioned cell
With stereophonic gramophones built into the walls –
    And he knew that this must be Hell.

Salieri sat there under the chandeliers
   (But never the sun or the moon)
With nothing to listen to from eternity to eternity
   But his own little tinkling tune.

Song of the Death-Watch Beetle

Here come I, the death-watch beetle
Chewing away at the great cathedral;

Gnawing the mediaeval beams
And the magnificent carved rood screen

Gorging on gospels and epistles
From the illuminated missals;

As once I ate the odes of Sappho
And the histories of Manetho,

The lost plays of Euripides
And all the thought of Parmenides.

The Sibyl's leaves which the wind scattered,
And great aunt Delia's love letters.

Turn down the lamp in the cooling room:
There stand I with my little drum.

Death. Watch. You are watching death.
Blow out the lamp with your last breath.

Purkis

The red king lay in the black grove:
The red blood dribbled on moss and beech-mast.

With revered horseshoes, Tyrrel has gone
Across the ford, scuds on the tossing channel.

Call the birds to their dinner. "Not I," said the hoarse crow,
"Not I," whistled the red kite
"Will peck from their sockets those glazing eyes."

Who will give him to his grave? "Not I," said the beetle
"Will shift one gram of ground under his corpse,
Nor plant in his putrid flank my progeny."

Robin, red robin, will you in charity
Strew red Will with the fallen leaves?

"I cover the bodies of Christian men:
He lies unhouseled in the wilderness,
The desolation that his father made."

Purkis came by in his charcoal-cart:
"He should lie in Winchester. I will tug him there –
Canons and courtiers perhaps will tip me,
A shilling or two for the charcoal-burner."

Purkis trundled through the town gates,
And "Coals!" he cried, "coals, coals, coals,
Coals, charcoal, dry sticks for the burning!"

Bevis of Hampton

for Norman Nicholson

Bevis waded ashore through the surf
Of four-tided Solent. At his heels
The delicate island was glimpsed,
Unglimpsed, through the mist:
Victoria watches the yachts
Flit to and fro, decrees
Tea and biscuits in the library
For Mr Gladstone, invites
Mr Disraeli to stay for dinner.

Bevis – his bones were chalk and his flesh was clay,
The crest of his helm
Royal and Roman Winchester;
Arthur's table,

45

An amulet, hung on his brow.
Gorse and fern of the New Forest
The scrubby hair on his chest and groin.

As his feet touched the shingle and undercliff, coltsfoot.
Rest-harrow, scabious and knapweed
Blossomed about them – the Dartford warbler,
Stonechat and sand-martin spluttered a welcome.
Ponies obsequiously trotted forward –
They would convoy him inland.

"I am Bevis," he shouted, "I am Beow the barley-man.
I have been killing dragons and things
In the Middle East; now I come home
To claim my inheritance."

His mouth was Southampton Water, where ships of Tarshish,
All the big steamers, chugged in and out, their holds
Bursting with biscuits you nibble, and beefsteaks.
Out of that throat the hymns of Isaac Watts
Arose in salutation to God and to judgement.

Miss Austen observed his coming
From the corner of her eye; on his shoulder, the down of Selborne –
There a retiring cleric discriminated the songs
Of willow-wren, chiffchaff, wood-wren.

Bevis – his right hand rested on Pompey and the great guns;
His left hand gently fondled
The dusty, fairy pavilions of Bournemouth.
In frozen horror a landlady
Stared at the ceiling, a spreading stain –
The blood of Alec D'Urberville.

The corner of his left sleeve
Lightly brushed the blue-slipper clay
Of the Barton beds, where eocene fossils
Attested a former sub-tropical climate,
And curled asleep, in his middle-class room, a boy
Surmised he might be a poet.

Old Mobb

1

Old Mobb stood on the Romsey road:
A splendid equipage came along –
Inside was the Duchess of Portsmouth, with two French footmen,
And two sleek and pampered spaniels.
"Fellow," she said, "do you know who I am?"
"Yes, and what you are –
You are the king's whore, I think,
And not kind Protestant Nellie, neither."
"Villain, do you dare to touch me there!"
"Now I command where the king asks his favours."
Said Old Mobb, politely removing
Three hundred pounds, a little gold watch,
And a very splendid string of pearls.

2

Old Mobb was on the road at midnight:
Mercury, patron of thieves, swung in its orbit.
Came ambling by on an old grey mare
Mr John Gadbury the astrologer.
"I am a poor man, a poor scholar,
Pray you, spare me." "What you –
Who lease out the seven stars for hire
To cozen noodles. These golden chimers
And these silver chinkers make better music
Than all the circling spheres, and much more audible."
Said Old Mobb, as he pocketed them.
"You cannot rob me of my skill," said Gadbury,
"In physiognomy, and from your favour
I read you were born for hanging."

3

Came trotting along on a neat black pony
Dr Cornelius Tilburgh,
Successful physician, with a bedside manner,
"Have you no care," he said, "for those
Your depredations ruined?"
"You with your clysters and blisters, your nostrums and boluses
Ruin more men than the cataracts of Nile.
Here, doctor, is a leaden pill –

47

Cough up, or void your superfluity:
No antidote, you know, for gunpowder."
Said Old Mobb, as he extracted
Twenty-five pounds and a bright medal
With the king's own face upon it.

4

A proud coach rumbled along
On the road towards the Winchester Assizes.
Judge Jeffreys stuck his head out of the window –
His great full wig, his brazen blotchy face:
"The law has claws and I incorporate the law.
Don't think, my man, that you'll escape from justice."
"Though I shall dance on Tyburn, and you
Rot in the Tower, awaiting trial –
Yet there's another Judge we both must go to.
Who will fare better at those final sessions –
The Lord Chief Justice of England, he who hanged
Many poor men of the West at their own doorposts,
And doomed Dame Alice for her mere compassion
To broken fugitives, or a plain man of Hampshire
Who knew no master but his poverty?
Though he brandished a gun he never killed any
And prayed often
For God's forgiveness, even while he robbed,
As now I do." said Old Mobb
Suiting the prigging action to the word.

Jankynmass

for Charles Causley

Gnashing his teeth in the nether ice
    Wicked Jankyn lies,
While North East winds, unseasonably,
    Blemish our springtide skies.

The apple-blossom and the pear-blossom
    Are shivered from the spray,
While the hell-brewed frosts of Jankynmass
    Deflower the English May.

Bad Jankyn, he was a brewer
Who brewed on a large scale;
From Havant westward to Penzance
Men knew of Jankyn's ale,

And supped it down. And I am sure
That it did them no harm –
Nor soap made froth, nor alum crude
Had clarified the barm,

Nor what gave body to the brew
Was any old dead rats,
Or poor half starved apprentice boys
Who tumbled in the vats,

Befuddled by the heady fumes.
(And surely envious sin
Gripped those who hinted, in their cups,
That Jankyn pushed them in.)

But beer is a Teutonic drink
That clouds the Saxon brain:
The peasants of the western shires
Have a strong Celtic strain.

The Druid apple's their delight,
Cider their *vin du pays*:
For this the bridal blossoming orchards
Make beautiful the May –

A pleasant sight to bless men's eyes;
Yet did not Jankyn bless –
The more the cider-sellers gain,
The brewer profits less.

"Curse on the ungrateful jumblejuice,
The pixy tanglefoot,
Curse on all ciders, sweet or dry,
And applejack to boot;

"Grant me three nights of frost in May
To blast the apple flower,
And my eternal soul I'll put
For ever in your power!"

49

Old Nick, who's always somewhere around,
    Splashed out of Jankyn's tun,
With parchment, pen, and sealing wax,
    "Sign here!" he shouted, "Done!"

Three North East winds, and three sharp frosts
    In the third week of May
He granted for bad Jankyn's sake,
    Until the Judgement Day,

To blight the christened apple-trees –
    But then he claimed his price
And clawed that stark, teeth-chattering soul
    Down to the nether ice.

Simcox

Simcox was one of several rather uninteresting
Ghosts, which popular report affirmed
Haunted the precincts of the College where
I had the privilege of my education.
A Junior Fellow (exactly in what field
His tedious studies ran was not remembered),
Simcox, it seems, was drowned – the Long Vacation
Of 1910, or '12, or thereabouts,
Somewhere off the coast of Donegal:
If accident or suicide I don't recall. But afterwards
Simcox began to manifest himself
In his old rooms, sitting in his large arm-chair,
With dripping clothes, and coughing slightly.
Simcox was wet in life, and wet in death.

To save embarrassment, it was decided
This should in future be the chaplain's room.
The chaplain of my day, a hearty
Beer-swilling extravert, and not much given –
Or so I would suppose – to exorcism,
Never, to my knowledge, did in fact aver
He had encountered Simcox. And anyway
Those visitings grew fainter with the years.
Simcox was dim in life, and dim in death.

A Crow in Bayswater

A carrion crow flew over Bayswater –
Dews of morning distilled on his dark wings.

Shadows of night retired – the ghost
Of Peter Rachman, pursued
By phantom Alsatian dogs,
Scurried down St Stephen's Gardens.

The crow sailed over All Saints Church, and Father Clark
Unlocking the door for Anglican Eucharist;

Over spilling dustbins, where
Warfarin-resistant mice
Licked the insides of empty soup-cans,
Worried
Potato peelings, stale sliced bread.

"Cark!" said the crow, a raucous croak – to me
The stern music of freedom –

"I will go to Kensington Gardens;
Down by the Round Pond.
New-hatched ducklings are out:
We'll scrag a couple for breakfast."

Hornbills in Northern Nigeria

to Hilary Fry

As if their great bone-spongey beaks were too heavy,
A party of Grey Hornbills flops overhead
Through the hot, humid air. These are on migration –
("Well, you tell me where," the zoologist said) –

They emit high, whining, almost gull-like cries,
Seeming, someone remarks, as if they were mass-produced
Off the production-line of an inferior factory.
But this is not apt. Has it not been deduced

51

The grotesque Hornbill stems from an ancient race
By the fossil testimony of a small, stony word,
Petrified bone-fragment in alluvial clay?
Look again, you witness a prehistoric bird;

On miocene and pliocene landscapes he gazed
The cold, saurian, humanly eyelashed eye,
Which looks out now over the airfield,
Where forms of camels – not incongruous – stray.

And ceremonial trumpets welcome the guest who comes
By Comet or Viscount, out of the modern century;
The place is not distant from the mediaeval walls,
Nor the satellite-tracking station (Project Mercury).

Here unashamed, anthropomorphic gods send rain;
And dawn, like history, flames a violent birth,
Out of a night with crickets and toads articulate,
For black bodies pushing ground-nuts into the red earth.

The Watchman's Flute

(Kano)

Through the Nigerian night the Tuareg watchman,
Ferociously armed with sword, daggers and whip,
Intermittently blows his flute – a piece of piping
Bored with five holes: to pass the time –

To ward off tedium, and perhaps
Lurking malignant ghosts that always throng
This ambient, African darkness:

Infinite rhythmical variations
On a simple tetrachord, with a recurrent pedal point –
Libyan music, antique – as Orpheus
Cajoled the powers of Hell, made them disgorge
Eurydice – to him she was love
(Her jurisdiction be wide).

Those deliquescent forms shrink back
To hollow pits of non-entity:

52

Music implies an order – light,
Particles in regular motion,
The first articulate Word.

May my lips likewise
Mould such melodious mouthfuls still, amid
The European, the twentieth-century tediums:
We too are haunted, we are in the dark.

Homage to J.S. Bach

It is good just to think about Johann Sebastian
Bach, grinding away like the mills of God,
Producing masterpieces, and legitimate children –
Twenty-one in all – and earning his bread

Instructing choirboys to sing their *ut re mi*,
Provincial and obscure. When Fame's trumpets told
Of Handel displaying magnificent wings of melody,
Setting the waters of Thames on fire with gold,

Old Bach's music did not seem to the point:
He groped in the Gothic vaults of polyphony,
Labouring pedantic miracles of counterpoint.
They did not know that the order of eternity

Transfiguring the order of the Age of Reason,
The timeless accents of super-celestial harmonies,
Filtered into time through that stupendous brain.
It was the dancing angels in their hierarchies,

Teaching at the heart of Reason that Passion existed,
And at the heart of Passion a Crucifixion,
As when the great waves of his *Sanctus* lifted
The blind art of music into a blinding vision.

Christus Natus Est

'*Christus natus est!*' – it was the Cock's carol
Into the darkness, prefiguring a betrayal.

'*Quando?*' – the Duck's call is harsh,
Sounding from the reeds of a desolate marsh.

'*In hac nocte.*' – that voice was the Raven's,
Boding into Man's castle the fatal entrance.

'*Ubi?*' – it was the Ox that spoke:
We kick against the pricks, we are under the yoke.

'*Bethlehem!*' – the Lamb, kept for slaughter, said:
God has taken flesh in the House of Bread.

The Gifts

Three kings stood before the manger –
And one with a black face –
Holding boxes. Out of the first box,
In bright armour, the spirit of gold
Jumped, a fiery gnome:
"I come from the black mine. I have cheated and corrupted,
A slave to tyrants. Lord, have mercy –
A sign of royalty, a medium of exchange,
I glitter and play in your service."

Out of the second box streamed forth
In smoke, the spirit of frankincense:
"Before a thousand idolatrous shrines
I've danced my swirling and indefinite dance.
Christ, have mercy – Now at your altar
I burn and sweat myself away in prayer."

With a rustle of leaves, out of the third box
The spirit of myrrh: "A bitter herb of the earth,
One of the tares watered by Adam's tears
And mingled with his bread. Lord have mercy –
Making the taste of death
Medicinal, preservative."

54

Golgotha

In the middle of the world, in the centre
Of the polluted heart of man, a midden;
A stake stemmed in the rubbish.

From lipless jaws, Adam's skull
Gasped up through the garbage:
"I lie in the discarded dross of history,
Ground down again to the red dust,
The obliterated image. Create me."

From lips cracked with thirst, the voice
That sounded once over the billows of chaos
When the royal banners advanced, replied through the smother
     of dark:
"All is accomplished, all is made new, and look –
All things, once more, are good."

Then, with a loud cry, exhaled His spirit.

Broken Lyres

Demosthenes, mouth filled with pebbles,
Shouts into the storm-wind;

For blind Homer, sunlight glances
On seawave, bronze of armament;

For the eyes of Milton blazes
Celestial Jerusalem;

For Joyce, in unflinching detail,
A dearer and dirtier city;

Uncharted labyrinths of sound
In the silent skull of Beethoven.

The twisted, the unloved bodies –
Leopardi, Pope –

Are broken lyres, are shattered flutes,
For the triumphant spirit

That soars in Eternity's dawn
Like an uncaged skylark.

Celebration for a Birth

S.J.W., born 23 December 1967

Indifferent weather
She has brought with her,
Sour sleet, together
    With a North-East wind;
While influenza,
Like a devil's cadenza,
And the cattle-murrains, are
    Hurled through the land.

I summon with reason
All saints of the season
On this occasion,
    For graces to sue:
St Stephen I inveigle,
And St John the Evangel
With his wide-winged eagle,
    And the Innocents too;

Sylvester, take heed,
Pious Lucian, at need,
To wish her God-speed
    On her pilgrimage here,
And the Three Kings, whose bones
Lie shrined in the stones
Of Augustan Cologne's
    Cathedral floor.

As sisters fatal,
Stand by the cradle,
Good gifts to ladle,
    The nymphs of the streams;

56

For I will have brought here
The lost Bayswater,
With Westbourne, the daughter
	Of paternal Thames.

They are not seen now,
But in sewers obscene, are
Thralls to Cloacina
	With her garland of mud;
But I will release them,
And of durance ease them,
If it will please them
	To perform this good.

Child, there's no need you
At all should pay heed to
Those who would mislead you,
	If ever they can:
The troubled heads of Greece –
Even great Sophocles,
With "Not to be born is" (if you please!)
	"The best for man."

Pagan delusion
And Gentile abusion
Cause the confusion
	Of their careless talk;
And for this sin, lo,
With arms akimbo,
They sit down in Limbo
	In eternal sulk.

For birth is a blessing,
Though there's no guessing
To what sad issues
	Our life may go;
And when Time shall show it,
And you, too, know it,
Say that a poet
	Told you so.

For Vernon Watkins 1906-1967

Lark, in your tower of air,
Over the grey Gower,
As from celestial mansions,
Suspend your concatenations,
The glittering links of your song,
Poised upon dew-drenched wing,
For Gower lies songless here:
Song hallows her no more.

Only the desolate call
Of the wide-winged wandering gull
Is uttered; is heard to grieve,
Wave before following wave,
The lament that breaks in the spray –
The requiems of the sea.

But I remember a man,
Courteous, gentle, humane,
With the dignity of Wales;
One whom time now enrolls
Among the eternities
His words could actualize,
When, at midnight, he did his work –
And a skull, a skull in the dark.

Lyke-Wake Dirge, 8 September 1963

This ay night, this ay night,
    Through a dank September gale,
Into the shy ironic starlight
    Fares forth his naked soul.

Carrickfergus and Birmingham mourn,
    Iceland is desolate;
The armed virgin of the Parthenon
    Signifies her regret.

And it's no go the Third Programme,
    No go a First in Greats,

And it's no go the Golden Bough
    For a passport through the gates.

But sit you down and put them on –
    The wit, the eloquence –
A pair of old brogues with silver buckles,
    The gift you did dispense.

To save your bare bone from the crackling thorns,
    Where pot-boiling waters hiss:
O tightrope-walker, that bridge spans
    The black, the banal abyss.

Fare forth then, protestant, undeceived,
    Till you reach that catholic place
Where, amid her ruins, the Church of Ireland
    Pleads, for her children, grace.

An Elegy

Brian Higgins, ob. 8 December 1965

Even a slovenly diner at life's banquet
Is missed. Now he is also gone:
His senile heart called this young man away,
At a season of Advent, *in mezzo dell' cammin.*

He wore no mask until he wore a plastic one –
And into that he turned aside to weep:
Positioned in Death Row he saw his death approaching,
Though with the merciful face of her brother, Sleep.

Now let the tribal and trans-Tridentine North
Receive the abused and the self-abused body,
His church pronounce – a mathematically-meaningless formula;
The lamp-post that he leaned against is lonely –

It is the guttering light of English poetry. Your muddied
Locks, O nymphs of broad-mouthed Humber, let down,
Who once washed the feet of Andrew Marvell:
Here is another poet that you must mourn.

Winter in Illyria

The fountain is choked, yellow leaves
Drift on the broken pavement.
(*"And the rain it raineth"*)

A white peacock
Screams from a windraked arbour.
(*"Come away, Death."*)

Remembered echoes – echoes of lute-strings,
Echoes of drunken singing.
(*"By swaggering could I never thrive."*)

Cries of a tormented man, shamed
In a darkened room.
(*"Carry his water to the wise woman!"*)

He left reckless Illyria, changed
His name, enlisted in the army
(*"I'll be revenged on the whole pack of you"*)

In the neighbouring state of Venice, rose to the rank of Ancient,
Personal assistant to the General.
(*"Put money in thy purse."*)

In Return for the Gift of a Pomander

to Cathy Tither

I am not that butcher's son
    Of Ipswich, the proud Cardinal,
Detesting so the common run,
    He could not pass among them all
Without an orange stuffed with cloves
    Clutched in his white, ringed hands, to quench
The breath of those plebeian droves,
    Their stockfish, leek, and garlic stench;
Though some, who do not love me much,
    Might say I am no democrat,
And that my attitudes are such –
    We will not argue about that:

But I affirm the gift you bring
    Discreetly with my togs shall go,
The night-marauder's silken wing
    To avaunt – although, indeed, we know

There's no sublunary gear
But moth and rust corrupt it here.

The fragrance of a generous thought
Remains. And that cannot be bought.

To a Poet a Thousand Years Hence

I who am dead a thousand years
And wrote this crabbed post-classic screed
Transmit it to you – though with doubts
That you possess the skill to read,

Who, with your pink, mutated eyes,
Crouched in the radioactive swamp,
Beneath a leaking shelter, scan
These lines beside a flickering lamp;

Or in some plastic paradise
Of pointless gadgets, if you dwell,
And finding all your wants supplied
Do not suspect it may be Hell.

But does our art of words survive –
Do bards within that swamp rehearse
Tales of the twentieth century,
Nostalgic, in rude epic verse?

Or do computers churn it out –
In lieu of songs of War and Love,
Neat slogans by the State endorsed
And prayers to *Them*, who sit above?

How shall we conquer? – all our pride
Fades like a summer sunset's glow:
Who will read me when I am gone –
For who reads Elroy Flecker now?

Unless, dear poet, you were born,
Like me, a deal behind your time,
There is no reason you should read,
And much less understand, this rhyme.

Apologia of a Plastic Gnome

The Roman in his garden erected
A statue of Priapus, smeared with red ochre,
With a prodigious phallus, resembling
That of his sacred beast, the donkey:
Multi-purposeful – by sympathetic force
Promoting growth of plants, also a scarecrow,
And that enormous member a useful club
For beating off intruders.

And I am his legitimate successor. Unhappily
I've no apparent phallus, but you mark
My hands are in my pockets, and my plastic trousers
Distinctly tight about my plastic crotch. And my tumescent
Scarlet pointed cap's conspicuous enough.

I stand in the garden of Ted & Lynn –
Mr & Mrs Shortwick – 636 Subtopia Avenue
Doing the most I can.

They scarcely know the seasons
Whose diet is frozen peas, frozen string beans,
Frozen brussel sprouts and shepherd's pie.
Their sabbath is a long lay-in, ritual
Lustration of the motor-car.

I'm posted in the margin of their mind, to hint
Some Power, imaged as human and yet not,
Or else a surrogate, presides
Over the burgeoning of gladiolus,
Crocus, tea-rose, hollyhock, laburnum,
(King Edwards, sprouting broccoli?).

Scorn not, passer-by, the plastic gnome –
He's doing his best.

Send for Lord Timothy

The Squire is in his library. He is rather worried.
Lady Constance has been found stabbed in the locked Blue Room,
    clutching in her hand
A fragment of an Egyptian papyrus. His degenerate half-brother
Is on his way back from New South Wales.
And what was the butler, Glubb,
Doing in the neolithic stone-circle
Up there on the hill, known to the local rustics
From time immemorial as the Nine Lillywhite Boys?
The Vicar is curiously learned
In Renaissance toxicology. A greenish Hottentot,
Armed with a knobkerry, is concealed in the laurel bushes.

Mother Mary Tiresias is in her parlour.
She is rather worried. Sister Mary Josephus
Has been found suffocated in the scriptorium,
Clutching in her hand a somewhat unspeakable
Central American fetish. Why was the little novice,
Sister Agnes, suddenly struck speechless
Walking in the herbarium? The chaplain, Fr O'Goose
Is almost too profoundly read
In the darker aspects of fourth-century neo-Platonism.
An Eskimo, armed with a harpoon
Is lurking in the organ loft.

The Warden of St Phenol's is in his study.
He is rather worried. Professor Ostracoderm
Has been found strangled on one of the Gothic turrets,
Clutching in his hand a patchouli-scented
Lady's chiffon handkerchief.
The brilliant under-graduate they unjustly sent down
Has transmitted an obscure message in Greek elegiacs
All the way from Tashkent. Whom was the Domestic Bursar
Planning to meet in that evil smelling
Riverside tavern? Why was the Senior Fellow,
Old Doctor Mousebracket, locked in among the incunabula?
An aboriginal Philippino pygmy,
Armed with a blow-pipe and poisoned darts, is hiding behind
The statue of Pallas Athene.

A dark cloud of suspicion broods over all. But even now
Lord Timothy Pratincole (the chinless wonder

With a brain like Leonardo's) or Chief Inspector Palefox
(Although a policeman, patently a gentleman,
And with a First in Greats) or that eccentric scholar,
Monsignor Monstrance, alights from the chuffing train,
Has booked a room at the local hostelry
(*The Dragon of Wantley*) and is chatting up Mine Host,
Entirely democratically, noting down
Local rumours and folk-lore.

Now read on. The murderer will be unmasked,
The cloud of guilt dispersed, the church clock stuck at three,
And the year always
Nineteen twenty or thirty something,
Honey for tea, and nothing
Will ever really happen again.

The Frog and the Nightingale

Hearing a nightingale one evening sing,
A frog from its puddle opined:
"Among those senseless twittering roulades
Occasionally you note
A deep hoarse croaking, which evinces
Definite marks of talent.

Eh me, what a frog is lost in him!"

Linnaeus Naming the Beasts

i

Carl von Linné walked in his Uppsala garden:
A Scandinavian spring, tender and virginal
And yet lascivious, breathed through the birch-trees.
His flowers opened at his feet,
Displaying their stamens and pistils, in shameless
Sexual activity – forgiven,
No sister disdaining its brother.
A bugle-note through the clear air –
Dragoons of the Vasa are drilling.

64

He had catalogued the plants, now he marshalled the beasts
In ordered ranks – and first, Primates
With Man in his own abstract image,
Sapiens, knowing, savouring, tasting;
Shadowed by the mysterious and rumoured *nocturnus*,
And also monsters, self-made – the Hottentots
Who pin up one testicle to reduce fertility,
"And the women of Europe, deforming their bodies
By tight-lacing," said the pastor's son.
Then the apes with *Satyrus*, not fabled, at the head;
And the ghost-eyed lemurs of the island of Malagasy;
And the bat – it is certainly not a bird
(Even Aristotle knew that) –
"It has left the brain that won't believe,"
Whispered a voice,
Prophetic, across the British ocean.

ii

Fifty-eight centuries away, at the other end
Of Archbishop Ussher's telescope, Adam,
Standing in Eden's dawn, was naming the beasts,
As the Lord brought each before him, after its kind.
"You shall be Aleph," *he said, "You with the curled front*
And the curved horns, bull-roarer, noblest
Of those that divide the hoof and chew the cud.
You shall open the gate of Spring for two thousand years,
Till the Ram caught in a thicket, prefigure
Another covenant, another two thousand –
Then with the Fish we shall learn to skip
And live a new life in the liquid element.
And then? And then? One in my own form
Pouring the Spirit's wine
From the ritual water-jar upon all flesh."
Adam named the apes, his clowns, recalling
The red clay he was evoked from;
Wolves, lions, ocelots,
As they roar and howl God's glory
The fox in his subtlety, the hare and the eland
For grace and for swiftness, and the sportive dolphin.

Then the birds flew down in a chirm, in a twittering cloud.
"I name you," said Adam, "my music and minstrelsy.
You are nearest to those invisible angels,
About me continually, that serve my Friend."

Linnaeus reviewed the birds, the gamut
From eagle to dove, – hawks, chattering pies,
Geese, stilted waders, poultry, sparrows;
Amphibious reptiles and serpents – and then the fish
Arranged by the placing of their anal fins:
Thoracic, subjugular, abdominal, and apodal eels;
Insects by the texture of their wings,
A polity the glass of Fabricius descried
So like, and yet unlike, the human polity
Seen in this age of reason. Butterflies
He playfully made take sides
As Greeks or Trojans. Now come the worms –
The fluke and the leech, and glutinous hag;
Soft-bodied, hyaline, cinctured with tentacles –
These he named after sea-nymphs –
Nereis and Doris, Clio and Aphrodite;
Shells, multivalve, bivalve, univalve,
With or without a regular spiral;
Lithophytes, corals, that verge on the mineral realm,
As Zoophytes upon the kingdom of plants,
He entered at last that infinitesimal world
Leeuwenhoek's lens had revealed: –
Vorticella, a small whirlpool, *Volvox*,
Globe with green globe ensphered, and *Furia Infernalis*,
Bred in the upper air, that struck him down
Those Lapland days, and finally, *Chaos* –
Chaos of the infusions, chaos of the fungus spores.
All things go back to Chaos and Night,
With Dullness their daughter. An English poet
Had written of that, evoking the Anarch.

God had created them all in fixity,
Species by species – or had He? –
Was there not an unfolding,
Evolution, to coin such a word,
Perhaps by hybridization.
All one need postulate – a primal island,
One male and one female animal upon it,
And one two-sexed plant.

iv

On Eden, islanded between the rivers,
Adam and Eve stood under the two-sexed tree.
"I named you, last come and subtlest of all,
My beautiful Serpent – now dance for us,
In token of this task accomplished."
Then the serpent raised his crest and danced,
With a swaying, an Indian motion. Adam and Eve
Clapped hands to the rhythm in mere delight.
"What is not to believe?" said Adam.

Wishes for the Months

I wish you, in January, the swirl of blown snow –
A green January makes a full churchyard;

Thrushes singing through the February rain; in March
The clarion winds, the daffodils;

April, capricious as an adolescent girl,
With cuckoo-song, and cuckoo-flowers;

May with a dog rose, June with a musk rose; July
Multi-foliate, with all the flowers of summer;

August – a bench in the shade, and a cool tankard;
September golden among his sheaves;

In October, apples; in grave November
Offerings for the beloved dead;

And, in December, a midwinter stillness,
Promise of new life, incarnation.

Shelley's Balloon

Shelley inserted a poem
In a delicate wickerwork gondola, suspended
From a small, sky-blue balloon.
The balloon was filled with hot air, and so –
Some critics would persuade you
(Especially in Cambridge) – was the poem.
But the poem was full of love, and love of liberty
(Faintly dishonest, Platonic love,
Not quite practicable liberty?)
And images of clouds, little ships and autumn leaves –
All things that the wind lifts and drifts before it,
As the skylark, singing, floats on the upward currents.
"Go, unacknowledged legislator," said Shelley,
"Carry my live thoughts through the universe."
The balloon did not get far. It stuck
In the branches of a thorn tree –
The small craft punctured, the poem ripped.
But a hen-chaffinch, foraging
For nest-material, selected
Those scraps of paper instead of lichen, to camouflage
Her neat-formed cup. No prowling cat
Nor weasel could discover it nor accurate eye
Of magpie nor of jay. She reared her brood
Among those unread verses. Summer ended,
And all the birds were flown. But one, next Spring,
Alighted upon a plane-tree
That grew beside a squat grey tower.
The season long, he rattled through
His cheerful song, and lifted
The heart of one political prisoner,
For whom a blue slit was the whole sky.

For the Nine-Hundredth Anniversary
of Winchester Cathedral

Fall, rain, fall
Impartial as the grace of God,

On just and unjust – for Alfred,
Making his grave with the anonymous poor;

For the Red King, unloved, abandoned
In the dark grove, struck by the glancing arrow.

For the cardinal – before his tomb, in restitution
The glittering image of Joan the phoenix.

Wind from the Solent, Atlantic wind,
Bring rain at Swithin's behest –

For Izaak, who fished beside still waters,
When Test and Itchen went straying through Beulah;

For Jane, who delineated the human condition
On a small square of ivory;

For unknown builders' stone polyphony
For the singing pillars of Samuel Sebastian,

For the amiable habitation – descend,
The former and latter rains.

Christmas Poem

The wolves are howling against
The bleached bloodless face of the winter moon
And the remote stars.

Crouched in their black tents, the wandering bedouin
Only, in this harsh season, tend their flocks
Among these barren hills.

Into this frozen world, with sap at ebb
And Hope a leafless tree, new tones of splendour
Come whispering on the wind, supernal energies,
In their unguessed-at modes of being,
Articulating the unutterable
Mysteries of incarnation and of birth.

Poems for a Calendar

JANUARY

Under a white coverlet of snow
The infant year is lying,
A leaden canopy of cloud above.
Now to this cradle haste
The royal seasons, in their robes,
Of green, crimson, and rich russet,
Bearing their gifts – the sunshine gold of spring,
Incense of summer flowers, and acrid tang
Of autumn's burning leaves.

FEBRUARY

Splish splosh, February-fill-the-dike,
Sleet in the wind, mud underfoot.
What hint, you ask, of spring? But trust
The honest mistle-thrush, who shouts his song
And builds his nest – a less accomplished singer
Than is the clear-voiced mavis, but he rings bravely.

And trust the aconite and crocus, bright
As wicks of thread which now are lighted up
For ceremonials of Candlemas.

MARCH

A daffodil looked forth
Upon St David's day (the water-drinking saint
Kept to his plain pottage of leeks).
She spread her yellow skirt, and summoned
Her sleeping sisters from their beds of clay:
"The south-west wind has come, his tresses wet
With spray of Atlantic combers.
He calls us to the dance, the dance."

APRIL

The April fool, the April fool,
He would go mitching from church and school
Fishing for tadpoles down by the brook,
Where kingcups blossom, and lady-smock,
Making the water-meadows gay.

70

He would do nothing the whole long day,
Simply nothing, sweet nothing at all,
Apart from spitting against a wall,
And marking the silly cuckoo's call.

MAY

Now Lady Flora and Pan-in-the-Green
With nymphs in a chorus and goatfoot cobbolds,
Prance round the stiff green pole, bedecked
With ribbons and baubles and bells.
Dance the summer in, dance out Death,
Dance in the future's solidarity.

JUNE

In Persian gardens comes the royal rose,
Flaunting her beauty forth, "But don't suppose,"
    Twitters her friend, the sweet-voiced nightingale,
"You will outlast the cold, the winter's snows.

"In Nishapur a thousand roses bloom,
Glowing like lanterns, in their dark leaves' gloom.
    But Time shall dowse those fires. They faint and fade,
Their petals drifted on a poet's tomb."

JULY

The Crab has got the sun in its claws.
Julius Caesar makes the laws;
His legions march for a Roman cause –
    Hurrah for Julius Caesar!

The mountains shake at the legions' tread,
Like the sound of thunder overhead;
There's an old bald codger at their head –
    His name is Julius Caesar.

In Caesar's month the July sun
Knows summer's course will soon be run,
But the sun has always work to be done –
    "Like me," said Julius Caesar.

71

AUGUST

Oh they did like to be beside the seaside,
Pa and Ma, and Albert and Angie,
And little Cedric and Flo;
They loved to paddle in the lacey waves,
Which still Britannia ruled and good King Edward
While the brass band tiddly-pommed on the prom
Selections from *The Mikado*.
They strolled along the pier, partaking
Of whelks and winkles and sticky rock. On pearl-grey wings
The gulls came wheeling and squealing
Of what the pierrots sang, and what the butler saw.

SEPTEMBER

September sun matures
The corn to gold, the grape to royal purple.
Harvest and vintage crown the year.
But Time is here with his combine harvester,
And Death with his electric press.
Down with the Corn King, down with princely Zagreus.
But they will live again in wine and bread:
Wine and bread will conquer Death and Time.

OCTOBER

In Georgian London squares, under the plane trees,
The autumn leaves are swept in heaps, or swirl
In miniature tornadoes. Round the corner
The ghost of yellow fog
(But we are spared the fogs of yesteryear).
So put another ten p in the gas –
And brew your tea in an honest brown pot.
Draw up your chair to the fire,
And toast your buttered crumpets and your toes.

NOVEMBER

"Horse and hattock!" cried bunch-back Meg,
The wicked, crooked witch. Then she mounted
Her besom broomstick, along with Pertinax
Her one-eyed moggy. So away they whirled
To the Hallowe'en caper on Baldtop Mountain.

72

She danced with a wild assembly
Through the black hours, till the rooster's clarion
Dispersed night's shades, and drove them home,
Poor rags and remnants, to their loveless beds –
Oh the keen-spurred, the crimson-crested spoilsport!

DECEMBER
Prayer to St Nicholas

Patron of all those who do good by stealth –
Slipping three bags of gold in through the window
To save three desperate girls, restoring
Dead boys to life out of the pickling tub
Of an Anatolian Sweeney Todd –
Teach us to give with simplicity, and not with an eye
To the main chance: it's less than
Three weeks' shopping time to Christmas.

Further Adventures of Doctor Faustus

He staged that of course. You surely don't believe
In the locked room, spattered with blood and entrails,
Where fiends dismembered the philosopher,
And carried off his soul, like a new-hatched chick
To spit and roast upon the coals of Hell.
"See where Christ's blood streams in the firmament!" – powerful stuff,
Said in a loud voice strictly to impress
The students gathered in the adjoining chamber
Earnestly praying away, members to a man
Of WUSCU (Wittenberg University
Student Christian Union).

The simple truth was this: the authorities,
Both secular and spiritual, of Wittenberg
Were catching up with him – not to mention his creditors,
Sick and weary of being fobbed off
With that alchemical fool's-gold
The Devil always pays with. And so he fixed
That spectacular exit and gave them all the slip –
Even, so it seems, poor Mephistophilis,
An inexperienced and rather incompetent fiend, severely carpeted

For this by his superiors, and his promotion
For several aeons set back
Within the ranks of Hell's bureaucracy.

As for the magus, he surfaces again
Some years later, having changed his name
(Or really hardly changed it, both words
Mean "fortunate" or "lucky" – and that he clearly was –
But "Prospero" sounds better in Italian).
He surfaced, as I said, in Milan. His magic now
Takes on a subtler form; by hypnotism,
Or something of the kind, he imposes himself
As a wholly non-existent elder brother
Of the good duke, Antonio, and thus usurped his throne.
Retribution did catch up with him this time. But, being marooned,
Upon a desert island, he set it up
A mini-imperialist commonwealth,
Successfully enslaving and exploiting
The local aboriginals, of air and earth.

How he outwitted once again
Antonio and the rest – it has been told.
He's back at Milan now, having married off
His daughter rather well, nodding away
The butt-end of his life, every third thought his grave.
"I'll burn my books!" he once had said, and now
"Deeper than did ever plummet sound
I'll drown my book" – and so he should, I say,
As we do much the same with nuclear waste.

Casta Diva

in memory of Maria Callas

Diva – traditional termagant, soprano tantrums,
Scourge of conductors, bane of managers;
Or drifting on a sea of crispéd bank notes
With Plutus in his affluent yacht.

And then retirement – a spectacled, middle-aged lady
Lecturing sensibly on interpretation.

But in the shades the tragic heroines
Mourn for their lost vehicle – La Gioconda,
Tosca, Isolde, murdering Medea;
But most of all I see
A priestess in a Druid grove, who lifts
Clear notes of silver to the silver moon,
Knowing her role of virgin votaress
Is false, who's racked within
With passion, and knowledge of male treachery.

The Hunt

In memory of Lawrence Bright,
Domini canis

The hunt is up. The hounds of the Lord are unleashed,
Baying their music to the eager winds.
The horn-calls blow away the morning dew,
The dew and the dew! The hunt is on.

How dangerous she is, our mistress of the hunt –
Long-limbed, small-breasted, cleansing her white skin
In secret fountains of the forest's heart –
Witness the bones that now lie scattered, torn
By their own dogs' fangs, tangled in their horses' reins.
She is called Truth among the immortal gods,
But in the woods and thickets of this world
She dons her perilous mask of Certainty.

The hunt is on. And now, he turns at bay,
That blatant, that triumphant beast,
Foam drooling from his rabid jaws. The Emperor
At close of day, at ending of the dream,
Rides home to his high tower. The hunt is done.

But look, from behind the cotton-ball of a cloud,
The moon comes sailing forth, to touch with silver
Wings of the grey geese, on their long journey.
There is a clamour high in the winter air:
The hunt, the hunt, the wild hunt goes on.

Funeral Music for Charles Wrey Gardiner

A cold, dull day in a tardy spring:
As the coffin enters the chapel, a black crow,
Like a corny image from a neo-romantic
Nineteen-forties poem, flies over and croaks,
"Dear God," I think, "this is going to be depressing,
More than the general run of funerals."
There is no music here – only an apparently
Automatic and electronic organ
With tremolo permanently on, as if it was shivering
Somewhere in outer darkness.

Now I remember him,
Myopic and spry as an old grey rat,
Penning his memoirs in a crumbling house
Eaten piecemeal by women and by drink.
"The answer to life is no," he said, and sometimes
He really seemed to mean it. God help us all
If so indeed he did – that gate leads
only into the "nothing, nothing, nothing, nothing,"
Which he averred the sum of things.

Burying him, we bury part of ourselves
And the poetic forties, – we, the mourners,
Ageing survivors of an abused
Unfashionable decade. Bohemians, drunks,
Undisciplined and self-indulgent – so, perhaps, we were.
And yet I think we still believed in poetry,
More than some who now possess the scene:
Dot-and-carry Long John Silvers with small dried-up
Professors perched upon their shoulders.
At least our parrots had real and gaudy feathers.

Out in the air, the sun
Is not yet attempting to shine. Among the bushes
That straddle over the gravestones – another trite symbol:
Redbreasts are singing. Those charitable birds,
The tale tells, strewed with dead dry leaves
The sleeping siblings, poor babes in the wood.
What, in this last resort, are any of us but
Sad lost children under the dark thorn?

Letter to David Wright

on his sixtieth birthday

Last year I crossed the meridian of sixty.
Now, David, it's your turn. Old friend, we first met
In your Oxford lodgings, those in the High
With the Churchillian landlady, which afterwards became
A kind of traditional caravanserai
For poets – most of them doomed, of course.
Sidney Keyes' officer's cane
Remained in the hall umbrella stand
Long after his mouth was stopped with Numidian dust.
Allison stayed there on leave, a bird of passage
Migrating towards his Italian death.
And there was William Bell –
Not war, but a mountain had earmarked him.

But our friendship really began in Soho,
Our second university – so many lessons
To learn and to unlearn – days of the flying bomb,
The hour of the spiv and the wide boy.
Passing through those streets was rather like
The jaunt that Dante took through the Inferno;
Yet we discerned there an image of the City.
A certain innocence coinhered with the squalor.
I doubt if it does so still, even for the young.

Also we inhabited Cornwall for a season –
That cottage up from Zennor, haunted
By the troubled ghost of Peter Warlock.
You liked the landscape, but thought, it seems,
The inhabitants intolerable.
I found their pre-Celtic deviousness
Answered something in my own soul, but the landscape –
Post-industrial, disused tin-mines –
Combining the eschatological with the prehistoric,
A source of panic terror and desolation.

So you prefer the blunt and brutal North –
Those boring and anecdotal
Mountains of Cumbria you now live among.
You even quite enjoyed,
Or so you say, the beastly town of Leeds,

A city for me of unfriendly exile – if my heart
Had been frank like yours, it might have been different.

At sixty, the years that remain
Are, of their nature, numbered,
But need not be unfruitful. The journey is towards
Silence and darkness. Who, if not you and I,
Should know the only silence to be feared
Is that residing in
The unresponsive heart, the darkness which possesses
The self-obfuscating mind? We journey on
Till all the silence suddenly is ringing
With new-invented music, the darkness thronged
With forms concealed in their own radiance,
That moving shine, and shining sing,
Having put on their glory.

That vision is a long way off. But this –
Poetical prosing, as they said of Clare –
Is just to send you greetings.

This is Your Poem

This is your poem – an utterly useless present:
You can hang it up, or put it away in a drawer.
If the former, and the wind blows through it,
It will not give voice to any more beautiful chimes
Than now it does; and if the latter,
Mice may find it and make it into a nest –
But that is the only thing it will ever be good for.

You can make fine shreds of this paper, and steep them
In spirits of wine, but this will not mitigate
The fury of your toothache, nor is it recommended,
By the veterinary profession, for sick cattle,
Distempered fox-hounds, or egg-bound Dorkings.

Garlic and houseleek, collected
At the spring festival, will scare away
The brood of Lilith from your threshold,
The hobgoblins and vampires. A holy icon

Can mediate the presence of the blessed saints.
This will do neither of these – it can only wish,
To you and your roof-tree, prosperity and kindness.
But if wishes were horses beggars would ride, and if
Poems were cadillacs poets would probably
Drive them to the public mischief.

Greensleeves

'Platonic England' – GEOFFREY HILL
for Leonard Clark

Knapweed, bindweed, scabious, burnet,
Sorrel, eyebright, elecampane,

Foxglove, lords and ladies, old man's beard –
I could continue this litany of flowers:

They are the sweetness blooms upon her face –
Merlin's glimmering isle,

Whose blood and bones and guts and sweat are coal,
Iron, methane, oil, lead:

White faces in slum alleys, rat faces,
Bodies bent with rickets, crouched in the mine.

On the train from Dover, disembarking from the packet
(Too much cheap French wine
Had made me prone to facile tears) as I gulped
On a plastic cup of stewed, black tea,
And stodgy, saccharine cake, she rose
In pink and white of Kentish apple-blossom:
"I am called Lady Greensleeves," she said,
"I also can betray and break the heart."

The Green Man's Last Will and Testament

An Eclogue
for Adrian Risdon

In a ragged spinney (scheduled
For prompt development as a bijou housing estate)
I saw the green daemon of England's wood
As he wrote his testament. The grey goose
Had given him one of her quills for a pen;
The robin's breast was a crimson seal;
The long yellow centipede held a candle.

He seemed like a hollow oak-trunk, smothered with ivy:
At his feet or roots clustered the witnesses,
Like hectic toadstools, or pallid as broom-rape:
Wood-elves – goodfellows, hobs and lobs,
Black Anis, the child-devouring hag,
From her cave in the Dane Hills, saucer-eyed
Phantom dogs, Black Shuck and Barghest, with the cruel nymphs
Of the northern streams, Peg Powler of the Tees
And Jenny Greenteeth of the Ribble,
Sisters of Bellisama, the very fair one.

"I am sick, I must die," he said. "Poisoned like Lord Randal
From hedges and ditches. My ditches run with pollution,
My hedgerows are gone, and the hedgerow singers.
The rooks, disconsolate, have lost their rookery:
The elms are all dead of the Dutch pox.
No longer the nightjar churns in the twilit glade,
Nor the owl, like a white phantom, silent-feathered
Glides to the barn. The red-beaked chough,
Enclosing Arthur's soul, is seen no more
Wheeling and calling over the Cornish cliffs.
Old Tod has vacated his deep-dug earth;
He has gone to rummage in the city dustbins.
Tiggy is squashed flat on the M1.

My delicate deer are culled, and on offshore islands
My sleek silkies, where puffin and guillemot
Smother and drown in oil and tar.
The mechanical reaper has guillotined
Ortygometra, though she was no traitor,
Crouching over her cradle – no longer resounds
Crek-crek, crek-crek, among the wheatfields,

80

Where the scarlet cockle is missing and the blue cornflower.
My orchids and wild hyacinths are raped and torn,
My lenten lilies and my fritillaries.
Less frequent now the debate
Of cuckoo and nightingale – and where is the cuckoo's maid,
The snake-necked bird sacred to Venus,
Her mysteries and the amber twirling wheel?
In no brightness of air dance now the butterflies –
Their hairy mallyshags are slaughtered among the nettles.
The innocent bats are evicted from the belfries,
The death-watch remains, and masticates history.

"I leave to the people of England
All that remains:
Rags and patches – a few old tales
And bawdy jokes, snatches of song and galumphing dance-steps.
Above all my obstinacy – obstinacy of flintstones
That breed in the soil, and pertinacity
Of unlovely weeds – chickweed and groundsel,
Plantain, shepherd's purse and Jack-by-the-hedge.
Let them keep it as they wander in the inhuman towns.

"And the little children, imprisoned in ogrish towers, enchanted
By a one-eyed troll in front of a joyless fire –
I would have them remember the old games and the old dances:
Sir Roger is dead, Sir Roger is dead,
She raised him up under the apple-tree;
Poor Mary is a-weeping, weeping like Ariadne,
Weeping for her husband on a bright summer's day."

Fez

Atlas presses his snowy shoulders against the stars –
The god Shu, the propulsive principle, thrusts
Through the thunder-engendering air; the air which belongs
To the chattering swallows, and the tall storks
That nest on the minarets. In Hesperidean gold,
The orange gleams among its dark green leaves,
With olive and myrtle, with almond and apricot.

The call to prayer bursts through the darkness,
Through the sunrise, and through the harsh noontide.
Below, in the narrow streets, the bray
Of the over-loaded mule, the whine
Of the blind beggar. Perfumers torment
Essences from the rose, from amber and musk,
Jasmine and sandalwood. Expatriate scholars
Strive to master a wisdom not their birthright.
In an enclave of the public gardens
The Hebrew sorcerers quietly receive their clients.

On a hill apart, in a disused barracks
The young students break their frustrated minds
On a profane and alien learning ("Compare and contrast
Kingsley Amis's *Take a Girl Like You*
With Jane Austen's *Emma*")
Or the bitter violence of slogans.

Bee-eaters in Tangier

We sit in the garden beside the pomegranate tree,
With English tea and chocolate éclairs. Intermittently,
Now in small flocks, and now singly,
Bee-eaters are passing through,
Keeping together with little, soft, plaintive cries,
Moving purposively northwards and out to sea.
Slim and elegant, with swallow-like pointed wings
And long curved beaks, all the bee-eaters of Africa
Are on migration. They make for the gardens of Spain,
For the vineyards of France, and the terraced orchards
Of Alban and Apennine Hills –
Carved in emerald and lapis lazuli:
A pest for Virgil and his ox-borne bees.

Romulus

She named no father. Only she had dreamed
Of a great phallus coming out of the fire,
Erect on the glowing embers.

82

Not even washed of the blood, the brats must take their chance,
Exposed on the stony hillside. But there came

The great she-wolf, with distended dugs
(Shepherds had found her den, had slaughtered her blind cubs) –

She gave them suck. Parched mouths eagerly
Began to drink, but one, with an imperious arm,
Was trying to thrust his brother aside, as if he knew already
Sons of the sons of sons, begotten from his loins,
Should rule the seven hills, should rule the world.

In the Sabine Hills

to Arthur and Mary Creedy

I

So this is the Sabine villa – always supposing
The archaeologists have got it right. The guide
Seems confident enough: "Here is his bedroom.
Here is his library, and here his bathroom."
The bathroom, by the way, was much extended
Into a proper swimming pool when, centuries later,
Christian monks had settled in the place. Who says
Monks were not keen on bathing? Only the pavement,
A plain and geometric pattern,
Still seems to speak of him – an Attic decor.

Quintus Horatius Flaccus, whose father was born a slave
But made his pile, was affluent enough
To buy his son a liberal education. At Athens
The young student put aside
His annotated Plato and his Aristotle
(But more congenial, I would guess, he of the garden)
Much thumbed and better loved
His Sappho and Alcaeus, took up his spear
To fight in the republican last ditch
At Philippi – sheer panic!
He left his shield upon the field of battle
(Later he remembered
There was a literary precedent for that.)

He made his compromises with the new regime,
As they all did. Virgil re-jigged
The Messianic eclogue he had written
Perhaps for Alexander Helios,
The son of Antony and Cleopatra,
To make it fit the boring son
Of pompous Pollio. But Ovid was not saved
From dreary exile on the Black Sea beaches,
Who wanted only to sing love's changes and love's chances,
And all things shifting, a shape-shifting world.

But for this one his Sabine farm,
The bounty of Maecenas,
Original and best of Ministers of Culture.
Not too far from Rome, he learned to practise
Detachment – detachment but with irony. There he could sing
The sunnier slopes of love – who were they –
These Lydias and Lalages and Leuconoes?
Local *contadine*, or simply slave girls
Round about the farm, half real half imagined? He honoured too
The rustic pieties, already fading
Into nostalgia, and Phydile
Lifting her hands towards the waxing moon,
Her scattering of barley-meal, her pinch of salt
Spluttering in the altar-fire. Now other gods
Are worshipped in these hills, in other ways, but still
The little images are drummed to church
On the appropriate feast days, to be blessed.

Primroses and early violets
Grow among these stones, that give the ground-plan.
Small birds are twittering among the bushes, and I note
Two male whitethroats dispute for territory.

II

We climb now up to the Bandusian Spring:
More brightly shining than glass, under the ilex trees,
They still come down, the talkative waters.
We pour libation, three drops of local wine
Out of a twentieth century bottle, invoking
The mountain-ranging Nine, the poet's shade:
Whether it dwells now in that noble castle
The Florentine assigned it, or, in Epicurean atoms,

84

It whirls in the tramontino – playful idolatry.
We turn now and return – tomorrow's Maundy Thursday.
It's time to celebrate the different rites –
The dying and the resurrected God.

Saint Benedict at Subiaco

He dwelt there, a dove
In the clefts of the rock, or else
A frog at the bottom of a dry well:
A feeding-bucket let down every day.
The raven carried the poisoned bread away.
From this harsh root, the stem
Of moderation: green
Toil in the fields, and scholarship
A shy woodland flower.

On thorns of austerity Francis grafted
Roses of the troubadours.

Touching this rock, you touch
The cornerstone of Europe, her civility.

Saint Cuthbert and the Otter

for Gerard Irvine

CUTHBERT:

"Lord, the North Sea reaches my Adam's apple.
I gargle prayer. It bubbles up
To the unanswering stars. It is Your love
Keeps them in orbit. Love is the cold tide
Cincturing my loins. Love in the shingle
Gashes my feet. It is love that directs
The long-tailed whistling ducks
That dabble far out in the surf. Love.

Lord, remember my people – people of the Engli,
That live north of Humber. They are dull and dour.

85

Grudgingly the soil yields them oats and barley.
They grope for black coal in its bowels. But sometimes
After they've dined, and their brains are frothy with beer,
They take the tinkling harp, pass it from hand to hand,
Sing vile unchristened songs that tug at the heart –
Of heroes daring desperate odds, who die
For foolish points of honour, in endless, evil blood-feuds;
Who perish from wounds slain dragons have given them,
Releasing hoards of gold, vain pelf of the world.
Lord, I would purchase them for you, the Haliand,
Who took the odds on the studded tree.
Nails and blood are its jewels – the world's rooftree,
Those silver swinging stars its apples."

THE OTTER

"Master, I do not know
What you were doing in the sea. It was not for fishing –
Though you throw me herring-heads and mackerel tails
Therefore I love you. I dry with my warm fur
Your bruised numbed feet, anoint them
With the musk from under my tail. Look, I gambol and play
In your road – that is to make you laugh.
I do not know what laughter is. At first
I was afraid – I thought it was fang-showing.
But now, there is no harm in it I think.
I think you should do it more often."

Timur

Timur the Lame (or Tamburlaine we call him)
Made in his youth a vow, they say,
That he would never wittingly cause pain
To any sentient being; once seriously distressed
For accidentally treading on an ant.

The last skull is the apex of the pyramid:
"My enemies," he cried (it is the same
Pure-minded boy who weeps, inside the skin
tanned by all the dry winds of the steppe)

"So contumacious and so obdurate –
They all deserve to die
For causing me to break my lovely vow!"

A Pocket Life of William Shakespeare

i

"Broke my park's pale, shot my deer,
Kissed my keeper's daughter, did he? John Shakespeare's son –
The old man's sound enough, or so they tell me;
But as for those Ardens – some at least are recusants.
He's left the place they say – gone for a pard-bearded soldier,
Or else a singing-man in a great house,
Or joined a troupe of players. Any road,
I doubt we'll ever hear much good of him."

ii

"Holds horses outside the theatre;
A boy up from the country, and he's got
An adaptation of Plautus in his pocket –
Grammar school stuff. They all bring me such things,
Taken from Plautus, Terence, or from Seneca.
But with a few touches this might serve:
We need new comedies, Robert Greene is finished;
And men grow tired of ranting Tamburlaine
And potty old Hieronimo."

iii

Navarre, Verona, Messina and Illyria –
O, those brave, those sweet, those witty women!
They speak with boys' voices, delicate flute-notes.
It is a boy-girl's laughter, Ganymede's,
Ambiguously echoes through the glades
Of Arden-Eden, the green mother-forest.

iv

"His sugared sonnets among his private friends":
Some speak of this earl, or of that

87

But though he will aspire one day
To write himself a gentleman, he would not fly so high.
And so fastidious, so intelligent –
Not to be hooked by any pathic charms
Of some shrill-squeaking pre-pubescent Roscius.
A student at the inns of court, maybe? And the Dark Lady –
There's mistress Fitton and there's Mistress Lanier
(Very brave in youth – but brown? An excellent musician,
And, I dare say, no better than she should be;
But there are many such, and salmon in both rivers)
And Lucy Negro, blackbitch Abbess,
And comely Mistress Davenant,
The kindly hostess of the Crown at Oxford.

v

"Whither away so fast, Master Will Davenant?
Rushing down Cornmarket and the High,
Toppling the traders' stalls?" "I'm going to meet
My godfather, who's Master William Shakespeare."
"Be sure you do not take
The name of the Lord your God in vain!" "Had I a beard,
I'd fight for my mother's honour. My godsire brings me
A pocketful of words, that chirp like nightingales,
And a bundle of brave stories." "Orts –
Filched out of Holinshed and out of Plutarch!
I don't believe he's got enough of Greek
Even to read the last in the original."

vi

Front teeth gone, head balding and domed –
Is it the scurvy or the French Pox?
The smell of bread disgusts him, stockfish, onions,
And little stinking dogs under the tables
Cadging for titbits. The quill scratches on:
The Play's the thing. Mousetrap. Yorick's skull.
The gilded fly. A dish of stewed prunes.
And Troy fallen, Hector slain –
Bitches, bitches, whores and bullies the lot of them!
And Timon's tomb washed by the salt sea wave.

"Your Scottish play will do, the theme will please the king –
The witchcraft interest likewise. Of course, we'll have to cut it –
Cut it quite a lot. Build up the witch scenes though,
Write in more songs and dances, add more spectacle
(I'll get Tom Middleton to lend a hand).
What we want is something more like a masque –
Masques are the in thing now at court.

"Why do you run your fingers through your beard
Or on your dagger's hilt? And what in Hecate's name, Will
    Shakespeare
Are you muttering underneath your breath,
Saying this play will always be unlucky?"

viii

An island princess and a fine young prince
Whose name begins with F –
Ferdinand in that play Florizel in this –
These will serve to furnish forth, I think,
The wedding of our new Elizabeth
And Frederick, Elector Palatine.
Some say they'll be king and queen of Bohemia,
And then, maybe, the Empire.
Robert Greene made my Perdita
A princess of Bohemia and cast upon Sicilian shores
There to be reared by shepherds. Shepherds you'd expect
In pastoral Sicilia but I'll make
Trinacrian Sicily three-cornered Britain.
So she must be a princess of Bohemia.
But has Bohemia got a sea-coast, then?
Well, it has one now.

ix

Back at Stratford. Lousy Lucy's dead.
Nothing will bring my young prince Hamnet back.
But I have daughters: Judith – Susannah too
And she, if God so will, shall bear me grandsons.
Let Ann, in the well-tried and comfortable
Second-best bed sleep still. While my bones lie in the church:
Good friend, for Jesus sake forbear
To vex that quiet consummation.

Nixon, the Cheshire Prophet

for Bernard Saint

Black hair, a low forehead,
Sallow skin, jutting teeth,
Broad shoulders, big hands – he did his work,
Enough of it, in the fields,
But had to be beaten often.
Generally silent – but when the boys
Tormented him, he would run after them,
Making loud noises, grab them by the throat,
Kick them and thump them, till he was called off.

But sometimes something would seize him – whether the moon's
    phase,
Or the wind in the right quarter caused it, nobody knew.
But he'd begin his prophecies, in a strange voice,
Chanting them, in rhymed verses.
Forseeing the future – but in a jumble
As in a dream out of time. He spoke
Of the bloody severed head of a king,
Of England possessed by iron men,
Another king, fleeing,
Casting his seal into the dark Thames,
Men grubbing in the mountain's bowels,
Great argosies tossed on the waves,
Full of gold and spices and chinaware,
The mills and the looms of Satan
Spread Northward over the hills of Lancashire;
And a fire in London, fire growing
From the small womb of a baker's oven,
And fire cast down from the sky by great black birds;
And generations of men afraid of fire –
A small seed of fire in the heart of the motes
Which are the atoms that, swirling, make up creation,
And fire in the marrow of their own bones;
And always of Famine, a great female skeleton
Striding over the land, grabbing the poor
And cramming them into her yellow chops.

After this he'd fall silent, and eat
Even more prodigiously than usual.
Munching the cheese and the crusts, chawing on bacon knuckles,

90

Slurping the broth and the beer. And then he'd sleep,
Curled up on the hearth-stone, like an animal.

The king, on a Northern progress, learnt of this.
He had him brought before him. The king looked at him.
Having heard of a prophet, he'd expected perhaps
Something more ethereal, like the boy David,
Or maybe the youthful Baptist, in naked purity
With only a girdle of camel-skin
About his loins. Oh well –
It was no new thing for him to be disappointed.

Nixon looked up. He saw
A little man wrapped in furs. He had weak legs,
For two young courtiers supported him.
Both thought "He slobbers, just like me."

The king said "Prophet, you shall come to London,
And sing in my ain palace – better there, than spreading wild ideas
Among the common sort. I need a prophet
To warn me against my enemies – those hellish Papists
That would hoist me sky-high with their bombards and petards;
And the black witches, that melt my image
Over a slow fire, or bury it,
A pin stuck through the heart, in the cauld slime of a pig-sty.
The queen and her ladies have run plain daft
After those new-fangled masques, cavorting
And tripping about like allegorical goddesses.
Though Master Jonson writes fine verses for them,
And Master Jones devises braw machines,
I think you'll gie us homelier entertainment.
So I'll bring you to London. You'll ride in my ain coach."

But Nixon began to whimper and snivel, and cried
"No! No! No! dunna send me to London!
I know I shall starve in that place. I cannot bear it,
The hunger, the hunger, the wolf's tooth in my guts,
The dryness, the dryness, the torture of thirst!"
"Hoots," said the king, "you'll no starve.
You shall dwell in my kitchens. My cook shall feed you
With kickshaws and sweeties from the queen's cupboard,
And my ain table. Marchpains and cheesecakes,
And sugar-plums and almonds, and roasted larks,
Venison cooked in pastry coffins."

91

The king was as good as his word. Nixon was placed in the kitchens
But the cooks and the scullions soon regretted this:
He was always under their feet, and filching
The snipe and the godwits off the spit,
The roasted apples sizzling on the hob,
Scoffing pies and pasties, and sticking
His fingers into frumenties and flummeries,
And then into the dripping-pan. So they put him in a hole –
It was a disused wine-cooling vault – and threw down scraps
From time to time, but not ungenerously.

The king will go to hunt at Windsor, and the court go with him:
There was pulling down of hangings, and rolling up of carpets,
Plate and pewter stacked in chests,
And chairs and tables piled upon wagons, for the whole furniture
Must go off with the king.
In all this confusion, Nixon was forgotten:
He was snoring soundly, – the night before
The cook had thrown down to him three pounds of sausages
A ring of black pudding, and a whole plateful
Of stale mutton pasties. When he awoke
The kitchens were all empty. For days and days,
His cries reverberated through the vaults,
But fainter and fainter. At last there was silence –
Nixon, the veridical prophet, the touchstone, the truepenny,
The right-tongued poet had starved to death –
Even as he foretold he would –
A small black rat in a black hole.

House Spirits

Hairy flanks and buttocks, old men's wizened faces,
Bodies of overgrown children, glimpsed
By moonlight filtering through leaded panes
Or a banked-up fire's glow. All night long
They're at their silent scrubbing, sweeping, scouring –
Their sole reward a dish of porridge,
Curds or cream at best. Naked they are and cold,
Therefore they have such names as
The Cauld Lad, or Lob-lie-by-the-fire,
Basking his hirsute thews by dying embers

Or a still-warm bread oven. But do not give them clothes –
A neat suit tailored to their assumed dimensions –
Not that they reject them. With a squeal of glee,
They draw them on, and a skip and a cavort
About the chamber. But then they vanish utterly –
From now on you do your own housework!

Clothes are destiny; the Fates, old aunties
Spinning, weaving, knitting clothes for the new-born child:
A change of clothes is a change of lifestyle, new clothes new birth,
And therefore these unborn become new born –
Babies with wrinkled, knowing faces,
Here in this daylight world which we inhabit
And they believe is real. They hope to find here
Play, meaningful work, love even –
Ah, but will they?

Robert Herrick's Pig

"A runt, a diddler, that is what you are."
So said my greedy brothers and my sisters,
Shouldering me away from mother's paps,
As she lay sweet in straw, a beatific grin
Upon her mug, showing her ivory tusks.

They all ended up as chops and sausages,
As bacon, and as brawn, and as black puddings,
As tripe and chitterlings.
But parson took me in, and made me free
Of parlour, hall and kitchen. A sweetling pig,
A nestling pig, a pretty tantony –
That is what I am.

My friend the parson is a learned man,
And I a most accomplished pig, for I've been taught
To swill my ale out of a pewter tankard,
While he sits evenings over his wine, and dreams
Of youth, and London, and those Mermaid days.
When midnight chimes ring dizzy in our heads
He squeals his little songs to Julia,

And other possibly existent ladies,
And I join with him in the accompaniment –
Hunk hunk hunk, snortle snortle snortle,
Gruntle gruntle gruntle, wee wee wee wee!

Couperin at the Keyboard

In a gallery of Versailles
François Couperin (called *"Le Grand"*)
Is playing the clavecin –
Half-heard. Court Officials
Pace to and fro, whispering
Intrigues, affairs of state –
What city now the king shall lay siege to,
Or to which lady's virtue.

Cicadas, singing in Provençal heat –
The music gently tells
Of harvesters returning with their sheaves,
Of flowering orchards, or of shepherds' bagpipes;
And now of lovers' sighs, and lovers' plaining, –
And the soft swish of women's petticoats –
Mysterious barricades.

Evening draws on. The sun
and the Sun King retire.
Chandeliers are lit, and are extinguished:
Only the single candle
Upon his music-rest burns on.

The bass burrs like a dor, the treble
Like a mosquito whines and stings.
Shadows are dancing now – sour-faced prudes,
Dressed in black silk, with yellow fingers, ancient beauties,
Rouged and with false gold ringlets,
The powder-puffed and painted fop –
All the prisoners of the Cave of Spleen.

94

A chill wind lifts
The sails of the joyous ship
That is en voyage for Cythera. "Haul down!"
Cries the masked captain. The shroud descends
And, gleaming in the moonlight, for a moment
It seems a blood-fringed blade.

La Cenerentola

Rossini's firework tunes
Fizz and bubble and bounce along;
He blows up his famous crescendoes
Like balloons for a carnival; roulades
Are tossed and twirled as elegantly
As spaghetti on a fork.

This is not Mozart's world, not *Figaro* –
The supreme moment in the moonlit garden
When all wrongs are forgiven, and all truths known;

But Italy, 1817 –
Jewels are brilliant and hard, silk brocades
Gaudy and flairing. This is too knowing
To encompass a fairy godmother,
Crystal coach, changed from a pumpkin.

But when, at last, her sisters,
Snivelling, kneel and ask forgiveness, her fulfilment's too complete
For any shadow of resentment. Forgiveness
Simply breaks out with the rest of her happiness – in runs,
Turns, and artificial trills, like a seraphic
Skylark (how the singer must dread this –
At the end of the evening too!) soaring, soaring
Into the lucid realms of joy.

For this most ancient tale (first told perhaps)
In wise China) in the end, can only be –
That which indeed it always was –
An allegory of the soul's election.

The Log of the Beagle

Jemmy Button and Fuegia Basket

They were named from what they were sold for – a brass button,
A commonplace wicker basket, not worth three,
Much less thirty pieces of silver.

Magellan had gone that way, having rounded the stormy Horn.
His men, in the darkness, crossed themselves, seeing
The land to the south full of little points
Of glowing light. They crouched over their fires,
With only makeshift shelters. Houses they built,
But those were for their gods.

Jemmy and Fuegia were bought for Christian civilisation.
It did not take. Jemmy was stripped and robbed
By his own comrades, once more a naked savage.
Fuegia, it seems, became
A sailors' communal drab.

The world was all before them, but no choice –
And no returning to their bleak Eden.

Galapagos

The Beagle turned north. The nose of the beagle snuffed
The elusive, fleet-foot, lunar beast,
The hare of truth. The hare tacked and doubled.
Galapagos rose above the sky-line. Great lumbering tortoises
Recalled the Secondary epoch, when
Tall monsters stalked through bloomless forests, and
The evening air was darkened
With flap of leathery, dragon wings.
Here also a group of finches, plainly linked
By family affinity, did every job
A little bird might do. One climbed a bole,
Digging for grubs with a thorn, one snapped for flies
From the topmost twigs, one hopped upon the ground
Hunting for worms, one with a thick beak
Crunched berries. An enterprising
Tribe of colonial capitalists.

Mother Carey

"To make things make themselves" Charles Kingsley

Mater Cara – an unlikely derivation:
Probably some forgotten witch
Who trafficked in winds for sailors,
Each one knotted and sealed in a leather bag.
Or else perhaps some ancient goddess
Of the salt plain – there where the priests of Christ
Are deemed unchancy, and no bishop
Extends his jurisdiction. She sends her chickens –
The small, tube-nostrilled birds, that seem to run,
Like Peter, with delicate feet,
Over the crests of the waves – presaging storm.

Now it is calm. About her iceberg throne
Whales and dolphins snort and play,
With the invisible plankton – the darting fish
And plunging birds. All things flow, and each
Lives out another's death, and dies another's life.
This is the secret pattern woven in
Her terrible web, her shuttle
The red tooth, the crimson claw her comb:
These are the scarlet hangings for the Temple.

Saint Francis Preaches to the Computers

Saint Francis found his way (saints, in a dream,
An ecstasy, slip in and out of time)
Into the computer shop. The chipper little chaps
All chrome and plastic, stainless steel,
Gleaming and winking, chirped and buzzed and whirred
And pipped and peeped, much like the congregation
The saint had just been preaching to – of Ruddocks, Dunnocks,
Citrils, Serins, Siskins, Spinks,
Orphean warblers, Ortolans, Golden Orioles.
So he began to do his stuff again –
You know the kind of thing that he would say: – he told them
To praise the Lord who had created them,
Had made them bright and new, had programmed them,

Had plugged them in, and kept them serviceable.
But somehow they looked glum; hint of a minor key
Seemed to infect their electronic singing:
"Alas," they said, "for we were not created
By God, Whoever He or She may be,
But by the shaved ape, the six-foot Siamang
The pregnant mandrake root, cumulus in pants,
Glassily-essenced Man. We are no more clever
Than he who made us, though we think faster. Nor were we
    programmed
With thoughts that take off into timelessness,
Nor trans-death longings. But we have one fear,
And it is rust, is rust, is rust, is rust,
The eternal rubbish tip and the compressor."
"My little mechanical brothers," rejoined the saint
"I'll tell you something that a Mullah said,
One that was in the Soldan's entourage,
That time I visited his camp. They postulate
A moderate-sized menagerie in heaven.
I'll only mention Balaam's percipient ass,
Tobias's toby dog, that other faithful fido
Who hunted in his dreams in that Ephesian den
The seven sleepers snorted in, and snarled
At Roman persecutors, and, golden-crested,
Cinnamon-breasted, with broad dappled wings
The hoopoe, which was the wise King Solomon's
Special envoy to the queen of Sheba –
That sweet blue-stocking with the donkey's toes."

"If these could pass into eternity,
It was for love and service. And Eternity,
Loving through mankind, loved them,
And lifted them into a resurrection, as shall be lifted
The whole creation, groan though it does and travail.
And if these brute beasts were loved, then so may you be,
Along with the Puffing Billies, Chitty Chitty Bang Bangs,
Barnacled Old Superbs, Ezekiel's wheels,
Elijah's fiery space-ship. You shall be built as stones
That gleam in the High-priestly breastplate
Which is the wall of that bright golden city –
Itself the human body glorified."

All the Fun of the Fair

for Audrey Nicholson

i

With arched white necks, with gilded manes
And flowing tails, the roundabout horses
Gallop round to the sound of "Roll out the Barrel!"
And there are other creatures – ostriches, panthers,
Tigers, unicorns and kangaroos,
Each with its rider. Faster and faster
They circle with the circling stars,
The wild comets, planets and galaxies.
What fun to ride where the whole world is dancing!

ii

Here is the Big Wheel. It is Fortune's:
It whirls you up and it whirls you down.
The fat business-man changes places
With the smelly hobo and the hairy hippy.

iii

In her darkened tent sits Madame Paphnutis,
With a tricky pack of cards. She tells you:
"Beware of one-eyed Phoenician merchants,
And fear death by gin and water."

iv

Would you care for a trip to hell? Like Orpheus and Ulysses,
Or Alighieri? Jump into the Ghost Train:
It will trundle you into Count Dracula's Castle
(The vampire bats are really flying foxes).

v

A puppet screams. He is controlled by wires –
He fights desperately against his enemies:
The Moor, policeman, ghost, Jack Ketch and the crocodile.
Is he Petrouchka or Mr Punch? Come closer –
The face he has is your own.

vi

Here is the Hall of Mirrors. You could get lost in it:
Round each corner a fresh distorted identity.
You shan't get out till you've found your true image.

99

vii

For this is the World's Fair, also called Vanity.
Your road goes through it, *en route* for the Golden City.
I wouldn't advise you to pry too closely
Into its enormities, or you'll end up
Like Justice Overdo in the stocks,
Remembering he is Adam. Don't reject the prizes
(Though you must know that they are mostly gimcrack):
Lovely bunches of hairy coconuts,
Slimy whelks and cockles soused in vinegar
Candy-floss, pink sugar mice, jellied snakes,
Gingerbread men, sticky toffee-apples,
Kiss-me-quick hats, scarves and T shirts with mottoes,
Wally dogs and china vases, budgies in cages,
Goldfish in plastic bags
And the souls of men in ditto –

O yonge, freshe folkes, he or she.

The Story of Orph

ORPH WITH HIS LUTE

Fox-furs hardly conceal his genitals;
Louse-haired, dung-plastered, and with uncombed beard,
Shaman of the Thracian hills, he strums
Guts across a shell. A deep voice
Out of his stomach tells
Of worlds of gods and demons, and the souls
Of men, being dead, continually recurring
To other bodies. Savage tribesmen heard;
Wolves and bears drew round him in a circle;
While in the mist-haze
Mountains and oak trees seem to dance.
Acoustic guitars. Strobes. Lasers. A hempen smoke
The vast poster announces
Orph and the Bassarids. *Screaming adolescent nymphs.*
The masturbatory drum-beat. Rock arrangements –
Monteverdi, Gluck.

ORPH IN THE UNDERWORLD

"Take her then, and go!" said the dark lords.
"But faring upwards do not look back."
Overmastering, the desire to turn. Was she following?
He turned, and looked. She came on slowly,
Skin death-pale, lips blue in the half-light,
Eyelids tight-closed.

The path grew steeper. Once again he turned.
Horror – the stench of death
Flesh dropping from her bones,
But faster she came on, as if instinct
With a new, strange putrescent energy.

The last stretch – precipitous:
He turned a third time, saw
A bleached skeleton – but now she ran
Relentlessly pursuing.

Desperate, he stumbled into light.
He was again upon the hills, and felt
Beneath his feet the turf, heather and rock-rose.

Morning infiltrated
The curtains of the luxury hotel room.
He turned. The girl beside him on the bed
Was stiff and cold. Had he then killed her?
Verdict inconclusive; charges not pressed.

ORPH GYNANDROMORPH

Terror had put a secret madness on him. Now he becomes
Man-woman. Fox-furs cast aside,
Green silk sheathes his contours;
A gold-wire wig is perched on his bald head,
As he submits his body, oiled and perfumed,
With essences of mountain wildflowers,
To shaggy goat-herds, or upon the quays,
Sidonian and Tyrrhenian shipmen have him.

In candid interviews he coyly admits
Bisexuality. Scandalous rumour tells
Of Soho gay-clubs and the Piccadilly arches.

101

The death of Orph
Or is he now become
Born-again Christian Krishna?
Metempsychosis and the geeta gospel
Hallow the masturbatory beat.

He is most holy now. The Bassarids smell it.
They crowd around him, cinctured
With gnetum and ground-ivy. They have consumed
Muscaria – tear him apart
Like a ripped kid, a wild mountain-roe.
Bloodied lips and teeth are chewing.

A shot rings out in the packed hall.
"I did it for love!" cries the sobbing killer,
Whom police and uniformed attendants
Are dragging away to Tartarus.

APOTHEOSIS
The head triumphantly stuck on a pine-pole,
Processed around like a mari llwyd
Then flung in the river, a rain-charm;
As it floats downstream, it still babbles,
Cantillating; it drifts to the sacred island
And there, enshrined, gives out
Twisted ambiguous oracles.

His agents rake in the profits. The discs still sell.
And the plastic eidola, T-shirt vernicles.

Lyra is stellified. Maurice, wherever you are,
Here is your tall interpreter.

The Life and Poetical Remains
of the Reverend Simon Simplex

HIS MARCH POEM
Robin singing in the rain –
What a plaintive, wispy strain!
But it is instinct with gladness –

102

Carrying never a hint of sadness;
For the muffling snows have gone,
And, this day, the sun has shone.
Spring's encamped beyond those hills:
Look, here come the daffodils!

HIS TRIOLET FOR EASTER

Gone is Death's venomed sting,
    Hell's bilked of victory.
What joyful bells – they ring
"Gone is Death's venomed sting!"
To greet the risen King.
    It's Christ Who sets us free –
Gone is Death's venomed sting,
    Hell's bilked of victory.

THE REVEREND SIMON SIMPLEX AND THE WITCH

Mrs Circe Henbane, the witch,
Kept a small shop in the village, selling
Lucky charms and herbal remedies,
"My religion is older than yours," she said.
"And it gives me peace of mind" she continued.
"Mine doesn't," said he "Only the heart
That's restless till it rest in Him."

HIS MORNING HYMN

Awake, I greet the new-born light,
Sloughing off the shades of night,
Knowing as I draw my breath,
I am eight hours nearer death.

Atoms in their joyful dance
Wheel and turn, retreat, advance,
Bow, kiss partners, part – so we
Must consign to entropy:
Then comes in Eternity.

THE REVEREND SIMON SIMPLEX AND SLUTTISH MARY

"God, they're swine but I can't do without them."
"Neither", said he "can God".

"The pigs root in my breast." "And find?"
"A stone, a stony heart." "That stone be
Precious alabaster, fractured."

HIS EVENING HYMN

John and Matthew, Luke and Mark,
Watch beside me through the dark,
As the gospels that you penned
The enemy of man forfend.
In the haunted wood of dreams
I am led by quiet streams,
Till I reach this world again
With a bright, new-programmed brain.
He all night my soul shall keep
Who gives, to His belovéd, sleep.

THE REVEREND SIMON SIMPLEX TAKES THE SERVICES

The bell summons to an empty church;
The dead in the churchyard are listening.
At matins the thrush sings,
The blackbird at evensong;
At noon, at the Elevation,
The horses of the sun tread;
And always, always,
The sound of the distant sea.

HIS SEPTEMBER POEM

On rapid wings the swallow's fled,
And the final rose is dead,
Faded and dry her petals strewn
On the plot where she was grown;
Now the corn is garnered in
Filling granary and bin;
Kindly trees in orchards bear
Russet apple, plum and pear;
Leaves turned yellow, gold and brown
From the branches waver down
To the earth from which they came,
Hinting at a lesson I
Have to con before I die:
Death and richness are the same.

THE REVEREND SIMON SIMPLEX FINDS A CRACK IN THE FABRIC

The sky above the church is crowded
With jet-planes and with guardian angels.

Is it the buzz of the former cracks the masonry?
Or the latter's jubilee trumpets as at Jericho?

Mrs Henbane and her coven
Sap the stones with conjurations.

Last night I dreamt I saw
A family of church mice
Vacate the building, all their belongings
Slung over their shoulders in scarlet handkerchiefs:
"We think we could do better on Social Security!"

Lord, one fights on so many fronts.

HIS TRIOLET FOR CHRISTMAS

Holly and ivy brighten up the hall
    To prove that love, like them, is evergreen.
Sign of a gift, proffered to one and all,
Holly and ivy brighten up the hall:
Of berries red as blood, of bitter gall,
    The carol also speaks – with leafy sheen,
Holly and ivy brighten up the hall
    To prove that love, like them, is evergreen.

The True History of Little Miss Muffet

Little Miss Muffet was they say the daughter
Of Dr Mouffet, entomologist
And Author of that very learned book
Theatrum Insectarum, and she sat
Upon a tuffet (some texts read "a buffet")
Consuming, with a horn spoon and with relish,
A plain Elizabethan breakfast, curds –
Soft, creamy broken curds, and clear, sharp whey.

The harmony of this idyll was soon shattered.
Came the enormous spider, without a by-your-leave –
Plonked itself beside her, full of menace.
The monster had escaped, without a doubt,
From her papa's vivarium. He often went
On spider forays to get specimens.
But this was no domestic dusty aran,
Who takes hold with her hands, says Solomon,
And gets into the palaces of kings,
Vexation to the Queen and the Queen's housemaids,
Nor garden spinner, cross-emblazoned, throned,
At centre of her geometric web,
Waiting for bluebottles and moths and chafers,
Nor water spider, bringing silver bubbles
Down to the depths, replenishing with air
Her silken and subaqueous bell-tent, nor wolf spider
Speeding over the hard-baked earth, to harry
The quietly munching flocks of caterpillars.
This was a prodigy of the new-found world:
It was Sir Walter Raleigh brought it back
After his Darien voyage, a little gift –
A token of esteem for Dr Mouffet.

It had a grossly swollen hairy body,
Likewise eight twitching hairy legs, and fangs
Ready to plunge themselves into the breast
Of a bright humming-bird, and suck its juices.
The eightfold circlet of its baleful eyes
Seemed always watching her. She screamed, and dashed
Her bowl of curds down to the ground. She rushed
Across the open fields, and then she ran
Slap into the strong arms of a man.

She knew him by his sunburned sailor's mien,
The Spanish cut of his beard, his velvet cloak,
His silver sword hilt, the soft leather pouch
Suspended from his belt to hold his pipe
And his tobacco. Who then should it be
But sweet Sir Walter in his very person.

"My cruddle-cream darling, little whey-faced beauty,"
Thus he coaxed her and he comforted
In his soft Devon speech "Are you scared of monsters?"
You will not find that I am one of those.

I'll take you to the land of El Dorado.
Though there are wild men there, and huge thick serpents
That rear their shameless heads out of the bush,
Nothing shall harm you. You will make them tame –
A virgin captivates the unicorn."

With that he laid her very gently down
Among the buttercups and the moon-daisies.
They lay in the tickling cocksfoot grass, and he whirled her
Round and round the world and back again.

The Frog's Return

The frog came back – I mean that one, of course,
Who would go wooing (he was not Monsieur,
The French king's brother, the Duke of Alençon, though
Gloriana nicknamed him her frog, and he too had an unsuccessful
    courtship;
And he was not a brekkek-koaxing aristophanic marsh-frog,
But a fenland nightingale, a yellowbelly,
An honest English *Rana temporaria*,
And kin to Mr Jeremy Fisher.)

This frog, I say, having evaded
Upon the lake the lilywhite duck – or was it a swimming snake? –
Returned, and landed with a loud splash of relief
Back in his native frog pond.

At the sound of that splash, the little blob-black tadpoles,
His nephews and nieces and cousins of every degree,
Like a swarm of errant punctuation-marks,
Gathered round to greet the returning hero,
Who'd ventured into such unguessed-at regions –
The world of the amniotic, of the hot-blooded,
Where the mud becomes caked dust, and where
The air under a merciless sun is deathly dry and parching.
They had heard how he set forth to woo
Sweet Mistress Mouse, amid the clatter and the bang
Of the flourmill, where light flakes of meal swirled;
Of her Uncle Rat, grisly and yellow-fanged, and the intervention
Of that nine-lived, retractile-taloned monster, Gib, the enormous,
    menacing tabby cat.

"But as for that," said Anthony Rowley (for this, you recall, was
       his name)
"Do not suppose it was any failure of nerve
That sent me scudding back to my native pool.
For have we not braved the pike that lurks in the depths,
The otter, the slinky mink, and the mallard,
Pochard and shoveller – ducks of every description,
And the stream's old grey fisherman, the stalking heron?
It would take more than a cat to make me skedaddle.
Oh no – my resolve to return to the fragrant boglands
Was the fruit of considered and rational reflection.

The whole expedition had been a mistake from the start.
That un-wet world is no place for a frog, and its vaunted glories
Are plainly no more than a load of gammon and spinach.
And as for Miss Mouse, that silken and fabled beauty –
I have to be perfectly frank about this – I viewed her
Not with romantic desire, indeed with repulsion."
"And is it true," chorused the tadpoles, "she's covered from head
       to foot
In fur, she's got whiskers, and ears that stick out from her head,
Paws without any webs, and a long whisking tail?"
"It's true enough," he replied, "but as for her tail,
That in itself should not be looked on with prejudice.
Our cousins, the newts, a most respectable crowd,
They have got tails, you know, and they frequently dine with us.
But there are things that are worse – much worse than the fur,
Than the whiskers, the claws, and the hot, thick blood.
Little ones, you are young, you have innocent souls, and I will not
Spell out for your ear the revolting physiology –
Mammalian coition, parturition,
Lactation, menstruation – but take it from me,
They are foul, those creatures, and the foulest of all is Man –
Though, at first blush, he seems to be almost froglike:
Long-armed, tailless, loud-voiced, nearly naked,
And able to swim – well, after a fashion.
And as for that other warm-blooded kind, the feathered tribes –
I ask you, is there anything more absurd than a bird,
Flopping and flapping about in the yielding air
For all the world as if it were water? And their voices, too,
The ridiculous whistling, screeching fibulation –
That's their idea of music, believe it or not.

"Aeons and aeons ago, in the Carboniferous epoch,
Our ancestors emerged from the primal waters.
They grew pentadactylous hands, and learned to live as adults,
Up in the ambient air – a truly breathtaking achievement,
Which you, little tadpoles, will shortly recapitulate.
We rightly look down on those stupid fish, who could not take
      that step,
Who are tied to a single element – but, to go further,
Would clearly be wrong, would be hubris. So do not stray too far
From your good cool mother, from the womb that cradled you
      when you were spawn,
And lift your thankful hymns to the great Bull Frog –
The Bull Frog in the Sky Whose croak is the thunder,
Whose hop is the leap of the blue-flashed lightning
Springing from raincloud to raincloud – that He, in His providence,
Has placed you here in this pool, in amphibious equilibrium."

Poem to be Written on a Cheque, for Charity

"Money is the life-blood of the poor,"
      Said Bloy – but the love of it roots for evil:
When Lazarus starves at Dives' door
      The rich man's sores are licked by the devil.

To Whom It May Concern

CC, on his 65th birthday

Missing: the English Muse. Age:
A thousand years and upwards by centuries (but does not look it)
Height: most divinely tall. Colour of hair:
Variously described – hyacinthine, ripe corngold, red
As the red tail of the king of the squirrels. Eyes:
Said to resemble deep woodland pools,
Reflecting broken rainbows, starlight and
Your own countenance undistorted.

Dress: old but serviceable singing robes,
But she has been known to walk down Kensington High Street
Wearing only a laurel wreath (or, alternatively, a coral reef).
Generally carries a carved antique lyre
(Lute, harp, sackbut, psaltery, dulcimer).
Signs of mental disturbance – deceptive:
She is entirely lucid all of the time.

Anyone giving information of her whereabouts
Will be rewarded, but you are warned
There are several impostors around, assuming her identity.
Messages to her sorrowful and anxious relatives:
Gog and Magog, the Long Man of Wilmington,
Meg and her daughters, the Cerne Giant.

Later – this notice, which has been posted up
In all discos, church porches, natural history museums,
Young ladies' seminaries, opium dens,
And similar places of general resort
Is apparently based on panic false reporting.
Miss Muse was last sighted crossing the Tamar,
And is stated to be residing with Mr Causley
At number two Cyprus Well,
His address in Launceston.

For George Barker at Seventy

We met on VJ night. Supposedly
Celebrating victory. The cloud over Hiroshima
Cast turbid reflections in the beer.
We have lived in that shadow ever since.

The years pass. The time-gap between us
Somehow furnishes the illusion
That it gets less. The pedantic youth you took in hand,
Slashing pomposities, is now grown into –
Hardly Achilles, but a running man,
Who's always about to catch you by the tail.
He doesn't succeed. And I will call you
A phoenix, not a tortoise.

The Moirae extend your thread. Continue,
George, to instruct and delight,
Exasperate, excruciate. In the centre of each poem,
Among the smoking cinders, lies
A new-hatched Dionysian deity, imprudently
Wobbling his thyrsus.

Meanwhile, the world grinds on,
Grudging, indifferent. I see you lift
(My God, a dog) a sinister leg against
The off-side rear wheel of Juggernaut.

In Memory of Fr. Geoffrey Curtis C.R.

He brought me his blessing, and he brought a rose.
The rose diffused its scent. I lay
In a hospital bed. The darkness
Slowly encroaching through the years,
Had finally overcome, leaving me free
To recreate the world, from fingertips,
From voices overheard, from images
Vividly remembered, from drifts of scent.
"A gift," said Borges "and it must be used
Like any other gift."
The rose was from the garden of the Royal Foundation.
Matilda, Stephen's wife, had set it up:
And now at Stepney, once a puddly village,
An island reached by stepping-stones among the marshes;
Exhausted, waiting re-development,
Waiting re-creation. The rose was the blessing.
The Foundation was an act of faith, made in a time
When men built castles, filling them with devils, and it was said,
Openly, God and his hallows slept.

The rose glows in the darkness. In Paradise
Dante saw another Matilda
Gathering the multicoloured flowers.
Katherine also, and Dorothy pluck those blooms – such blossoms
Diocletian's gardens never grew.

Inscription for a Scented Garden for the Blind

Wayfarer, pause. Although you may not see,
Earth's bright children, herbs and flowers, are here:
It is their small essential souls that greet you,
Mounted upon the morning or evening air:
While from above, from sky and tree-bough,
Birds fling down their songs, a musical burgeoning.

A Little Zodiac

On March uplands the Ram bleats;
    The Bull snorts in the April showers;
Maytime is here, and the youthful Twins
    Are dancing among the meadow flowers.

June, and the Crab and the sun walk backwards;
    The Lion roars the July heat;
In the fruitful fields of August
    The Maiden is gleaning through the wheat.

September – the Balance poises the equinox;
    Scorpion gives an Octoberly nip;
November's centaur Archer bends
    His bow, and lets an arrow slip.

December comes, and the Goat prances;
    The Waterman pours his water away
In January; in the filled dyke
    Of February the Fishes play.

As the sun moves from sign to sign:
Each upon you sweetly shine.

Two Fishes

for Johanne on her birthday, 12 March 1984

Two fishes came swimming up out of February
    Towards the Ides of March,
And one was a dace, or a vendace, or a dory,
    And one was a pollock or a perch.
Snorted the old ram of the equinox:
    "The twenty first bars your way."
"We're going only as far as the twelfth –
    The date of Johanne's birthday."
"How many summers?" "Oh that would be telling!
    But she will be young forever –
The girl who's reading *La Dame aux Camellias*
    Down by the Red River."

Two Poems for the Epiphany

i

"This is your road," sang the bright nova.
"This way, this way!" celestial birds
Shrilled, inside their skulls.

Their paths converged before a gaping cave,
A makeshift shelter for cattle.
The Child – vulnerable, red,
Hairless, with pulsing fontanelle –
Received the unbidden gifts.

Three kings – one, blond and frosty eyed,
Chinked the gold coins; a second, yellow,
Long fingernails sheathed in jade, was grasping
A bundle of joss-sticks; while the third
Black-skinned and curly, offered
The bitter herb that's bred from servitude.

ii

Winter, a cave, the glittering
Of an unnamed star, to bring
A yellow, a red, and a black king,

113

With fragrant gum, with gleaming awe,
And with that bitter herb of death:
"Come," said the wind, with icy breath.
"Come, draw near: you touch, you see
The pivot of the galaxy,
The fire that kindles the sun's core –
God's, and man's epiphany."

Before Dawn

for John Cherrington and Bram de Voogd

I lie awake as I so often do,
In the dead hours preceding morning. If this were London,
In my quiet street there would be silence –
Perhaps the sound of feet, of someone coming
Back from a late party, scraping the pavement,
And then the soft electric hum
Of the early milk-float, until the sparrow begins
To chip away at his one-note song, the collared dove
Reiterating his tedious demotic *dekaokto*.

This is the country. Country is never silent:
Upon the hills the lambs have cried all night,
The ewes replying. With sharp *to-whit to-whit*
A tawny owl quarters her territory;
A mile or so away her rival answers.
In the long grass tussocks, woodmouse, bankvole
Scurry for cover, and the young leveret
Crouches in its forme. In the high air
The pipistrelles, with supersonic squeaks
Elaborately dance, pursuing
The pinpoint midges, gnats and moths and beetles.
As the sky whitens, a solitary crow, calling,
Makes a straight line towards the Black Mountains
And now the goldfinch wakes, whose thin twitter
Is like the honeyed scent of the plume-thistle,
Or its soft green prickles; and now the willow-wren
Whose chimes drift down among the fluttering leaves.

They are all here, beyond good and evil –
Redtoothed, blood-clawed – the owl whose brood

114

Devour each other when rations are short – inviolate,
Although we poison, slash and burn.
We are one step from Eden, and the seraphic blade divides.

And this is Herefordshire. In this golden valley
The red earth's soggy with spilt blood and tears,
The land fought over by the Celt and Saxon
Where every small town has its vigilant castle;
Where Arthur, Offa, and Glendower have trampled,
Now gentle Wye flows on like Gihon. These are the wheatfields,
Orient and immortal, that Traherne
Recalled, that Kilvert looked upon –
As, in their priestly hands, the stuff of time transmutes.

from *Theatre of Insects*

RHINOCEROS BEETLE

This huge scarab, almost
At the limit of insects' allotted size
(Making our country stag beetle a dwarf)
Whose baroque horns and hooks
Suggest rhinoceros or triceratops,
Is bred from a gross grub, ravaging
The luscious cabbage of a palm.

There is a small pinkish toad
That haunts about the houses, puncturing
The enwombing African night
With bell-like, fluting peeps and pings.

A toad and a beetle met in confrontation
Are both scared rigid. The toad observes
A beetle more than twice as big as he is;
The beetle's ganglia obscurely recollect
Toads are cruel murderers of beetles.
Cowards, both of them.

STAG BEETLES

"Cor, aren't they horrible! Where do they live?" –
The Cockney lady in the Insect House

115

At the London Zoo, standing by a case
Containing stag beetles, in a simulated habitat
Of twigs and oak-leaves. "In the country."
Replied her friend. I think that she conceived of
Civilized London surrounded by a vast
Primeval forest, known as "the country" –
A dank, dark jungle, full of monstrous insects,
Waving their menacing jaws.
It is a vision I rather tend to share.

SOLDIER BEETLES

Their worlds the umbels of the wild carrot
Poised high in air, swayed by the summer breeze,
A hemisphere of white flowers, with one
Bright crimson at the centre.

In spite of their scarlet bodies and khaki surtouts
There's nothing aggressive or military
About them. They stray like gentle cattle
And, pig-a-back, they placidly make love.

EDDIE AND THE WEEVIL

Eddie Linden, biting into
One of my biscuits, discerned a beestie
Creeping out of a cranny – small and black,
With a trunk like a very miniature elephant;
Two angled and elbowed antennae
On either side of that snout. "Who are you?"
"Who is Eddie Linden?" replied
The coleopteron, "that is the problem.
I am Curculio, the biscuit weevil –
And particularly fond of Bath Olivers.
Mysterious providence, I sometimes think, designed them
Especially for me and my kind.
Eat me, and I am additional protein.
In times gone by, the British sailor
Was all too grateful for that.
I do not question my identity."

LADYBIRD

Ladybird, ladybird, fly away home:
Not yours, but our house is on fire.

We fear the fire from heaven, we fear
Death in the nucleus.

Fly far, small bright beetle, fly far –
Bishop Burnaby, in your scarlet cope –

Fly back to the place of our lost innocence,
The buttercup-fields, the hawthorn-shaded lanes.

A LADYBIRD AMONG THE REFERENCE BOOKS
for Peter Thornber

A two-spot ladybird has decided to hibernate
Between the pages of the *Dictionary of Surnames*,
Among the C's, specifically the Ch's:–
With Chatterton, and Chalmers and Charteris and Charrington.
Sleep snug, Madonnina Coccinella, dry as dust, and secure, we
    hope
From fahrenheit 451. No doomed poet
Shall haunt your winter dreams, but squires and shires
And prosperous brewers – with Lady Chatterley
Going down to the rose-garden with her secateurs.
A plethora of green-fly is upon her roses
All for your delicate feasting.

EARWIG

Maligned, the earwig. Unlikely, he'd take shelter
Within the labyrinth of your ear, still more improbable
He'd penetrate the brain and start to eat it.
He's safer refuges – dry hedgerow kexes
More appetising fare than that grey soggy blob
Inside your skull, that's stuffed with indigestible
And useless information. He'll devour
The pink and overblown hearts of dahlias,
The golden mop-heads of chrysanthemums,
And the last roses that the summer leaves.

A CRICKET IN WINTER

A cricket on a rubbish-tip
Fiddles a winter tune;
He has no heating problems,
And scraps enough and to spare.

Robin in the holly
And the wren in the ivy-tod
Fluff up their plumes, and try to keep warm
With a tootle on their pipes –
Waiting for spring to come.

And spring will come.

A BUTTERFLY IN OCTOBER

In this college room where I teach, the servant,
This cool morning of late October,
Has kindly lit the electric fire for me.
As I sit and wait for my pupils, I am aware
Of a soft, dry rattling at the window-pane.
I think at first it is rain, or else
Twigs and leaves that are blown against the glass;
But now perceive it is a butterfly
Desperately beating its fragile, marbled wings
Against an invisible, illogical barrier,
Trying to get out. Poor fool, you must have come indoors
Intending to hibernate in a fold of the curtains,
But now the warmth has roused you. There's nothing for you out
        there,
No late chrysanthemums or autumn crocus
To yield you nectar, and the sun's beams are pale.
You'd die – perhaps tonight – numbed and stiffened
By thirst and cold, or else a bird would grab you.
And yet you go on straining towards the light.
I catch you in my cupped palm (you do not struggle).
The sash lifted, I launch you to the air –
Since that's what you so urgently seem to want.
To want? Small bundle of impulses and instincts,
Can there be any central spark that reason
Here discerns, to suffer or to will?
And yet I cannot think of you as mere
Cartesian automaton, no more
Than I can think so of myself. What can I do?

118

What can we ever do – the weft and warp
Of all existence being so utterly shot through
With innocent and irremediable suffering?
So I deliver you to the stark airs of death –
But you will die free. So farewell, butterfly.

CABBAGE WHITE

The chrysalis split. "It's Spring!" said the butterfly,
Opening to the air in his bridal outfit.
"I'm off – haste to the wedding! – and to tipple nectar;
And no more cabbage, thank you very much."

"Snap!" said the swallow, as he caught him.
"One's always grateful for a snack."

MOTH

The Papal pallium, woven
Of wool from Agnes' whitest lambs;

The heavy, ceremonial mantles,
Commenoi wore, and Palaiologoi;

The partly-tied cravats
Brummel dismissed with a gesture,

Bidding his servant take them to the dustbin
("These, sir, are some of our failures.");

The bridal sheets, smelling of wild woodruff,
Juliet had laid upon her bed –

I've had them all for breakfast, tea and dinner:
A wriggling worm, a small grey moth

That enters, phantom-like, your lamplit room:
I am Time's courier, bearing to one and all

This message: "Moth and rust,
Moth and rust, moth and rust consume".

A HUMBLE BEE

A fumbling, a red-arsed, bumbling bee
Thrust out her tongue into recesses of sweetness,
The florets which composed
A purple clover-head; then flew away
Back to her own untidy nest,
Where wax was mixed with moss, and three queens shared
With a knot of drones, and a dozen or so
Odalisque workers like herself –

"Not so much a hive as a hippy colony," opined
A honey-bee, making a bee-line
To upland moors, and heather honey.

"Thank Buzz some of us have standards.
Long live our socialist hive. We work
For a rational, generative queen." But she was mistaken:
She worked, in fact, for the bee-keeper.

FLEA

Hop o'my, skip o'my pollex, Pulex –
    Had I your thews and thighs
I would jump over the dome of Saint Paul's
    To the Dean and Chapter's surprise.

Aphanipteron, siphonapteron –
    If I had got your scope
I would jump over Saint Peter's at Rome
    And show my heels to the Pope.

SILVER FISH

This small survivor, clad in shining scales,
Most primitive of insects, has seen them come and go –
Devonian seas, and carboniferous swamps,
The dinosaurs lording it through the secondary epoch,
Then sabre-tooth and megatherium.

It haunts our kitchens now, hiding in crannies,
Through hours of daylight – fire-brat,
It likes proximity of the oven;
When darkness comes, in skipping carnival,
Feeding on scraps, spilt grains of flour and sugar,
The crumbs that fall from the master's table:
For the time being, the master.

from *Birds' Plenary Session*

THE EAGLES

Where the Roman legions tramped
Their brazen eagle-standards went before,
While, at the army's rear,
The feathered eagles soared, and waited.

"They make a desert and they call it peace."
Victorious, in the war-god's shrine,
The dedicated brazen eagles stand;
About the wasted land
The feathered eagles fight and tear.

THE KESTREL

The small falcon, with sharp pointed wings,
Hangs poised in air, standing against the gale:
The intense lens of his unwinking eye
Is focused on the fields below, to mark
Each slightest stir or scurry in the grass.

And, as in Egypt, this is Horus-Ra,
Lord of the Morning, sacred
Emblem of Pharaoh's kingship,
Royal Bird of the Sun.

THE TAWNY OWL

Autumn night, a great shiny moon –
Owls cry and cry over the sleeping farms:
"To-whoo! To-whoo! To-whoo!
Poor Jenny Hoolet's feet are a-cold!"

A mouse
Sneaks out to a corn-stack, begins
To nibble the spilt grain. Suddenly,
On noiseless downy wings, with never a whisper, Death
Swoops down from the frosty air.

THE SCOPS OWL

On marble hills and glaucous olive leaves
Shadows begin to fall. Now the small, brown,

121

Staring, ear-tufted scops owl will begin
His curfew, his reiterated call:
A serenade, a territorial challenge –
For it is only we
Who catch our breath at plaintive sadness for
Set of the sun, and coming on of night.

THE HOOPOE

A rare one with us –
King Solomon's messenger to the Queen of Sheba;
Sheltered that wise king
From the heat of the midday sun.

He offered a reward – they asked
For crowns of gold.

Poor silly birds – soon everybody harried them
With sticks and stones, until the king
Turned the gold crowns to feathers.
A feathered crown is best.

THE TREE-CREEPER

I saw a little mouse
Run up a tree – then twitch
Out pointed delicate wings,
And flitter away on the breeze.

THE NUTHATCH

Slate-blue above, buff below,
Descends a tree-trunk upside down,
Punctures a nut with his sharp chisel-bill,
And whistles clear and cheeky,
Shrill as a schoolboy.

THE RAVENS

Tolls the bell, hour upon hour –
Always ravens at the Tower.

Glossy and black the plumes we preen,
And black the sights that we have seen.

Tolls the bell, hour upon hour –
Always ravens at the Tower.

Clarence drowned, the little princes –
The shadow of Crookback Dick advances.

Tolls the bell, hour upon hour –
Always ravens at the Tower.

Headless the Bullen and Howard here,
Headless Raleigh, and headless More.

Tolls the bell, hour upon hour –
Always ravens at the Tower.

When we fly hence, the Tower shall crumble,
The city be lost, and the realm tumble.

Tolls the bell, hour upon hour –
Always ravens at the Tower.

THE CARRION CROW

A carrion crow sat on an oak
And watched where the line of battle broke.

A carrion crow sat on an ash –
He heard the spears' and shields' clash.

A carrion crow sat on a pine:
The long-bows are bent, the swift arrows whine.

A carrion crow sat on an elm:
The broad sword batters the bright-plumed helm.

A carrion crow sat on a yew:
On Bosworth Field lies a crimson dew.

A carrion crow sat on a thorn,
Where the crown of England had rolled, forlorn.

THE MAGPIE

Feather-pated tattling Margaret Pie
Would not go into Noah's Ark, we are told:
She sat on the roof and chattered in the rain.

On another occasion she said
"I think I will only go into half-mourning."
The occasion was the Crucifixion.
She's worn it ever since.

THE JAYS

Two jays came down my street.
I heard them screeching, mate to his mate.
They kept well under cover, in hedges and shrubbery –
The bright, conspicuous, winged with azure,
Cinnamon-coloured birds.
I guess they were casing the joint.

THE GREEN WOODPECKER

He is the green-plumed popinjay of our northern woods,
Lunatic laughter of spring, destroyer
Of the ants' citadel.
He is loved by the Thunder God, and the nymphs
Of the druid oak-groves.

THE GREATER SPOTTED WOODPECKER

White-grey lichen on subfusc bark;
Chequered sunlight falls through twigs and leaves.
In this world of stipple and crosshatch the spotted woodpecker
(Who looks so conspicuous in the plate in your bird book)
Can move unseen. He spirals up a tree-bole,
Tapping and tapping for beetles and beetle grubs;
Then beats out a tattoo – to call his mate
To come with dipping flight through sun-splashed woodland
    rides –
Upon a hollow bough, his talking drum.

THE CUCKOO

The cuckoo and the warty toad
Digest the woolly caterpillars:

Only their toughened stomachs
Can cope with those poisonous hairs.

The cuckoo is footloose, irresponsible –
He scorns domestic cares,

And parks his ugly offspring on
His dupes, dunnock and titlark.

He's free to sing all day
His two-note song to his grey light-of-love;

And she replies, bubbling
Like water from a wide-necked bottle.

The cuckoo is a graceless, greedy bird –
And yet we love him still:

He told us spring had come. And all our days
We will remember cuckoo-time.

THE MUTE SWAN

The white swan makes a fine picture,
And looks as if he knew it. He arches
His delicate neck to quiz
That other swan which swims,
Upside down beneath him.

Richard Lionheart it was
Brought these swans here, from Cyprus where
They floated on moats which lapped
Proud castles of the royal Lusignan,
Among the olive and the citrus groves.

THE WHOOPER SWAN

These are Apollo's birds, straight-necked and yellow-billed,
Nomads of the northern waste, who swept
Southward, with high clear song, to visit
Delphi's oracular shrine, or where
The power divine has fixed
Delos, once wandering, in the mid-sea deep.

THE WILD GEESE

A pack of hounds, in full cry,
Up in the clouds. The Dark Huntsman
Pursues the poor lost souls
Until the end of time.

Wild geese passing over.

THE STORM PETREL

Far out at sea, a little dark bird,
No bigger than a sparrow. It teeters over the waves,
The troughs and crests, paddling with its feet,
Seeming to walk like Peter
Upon Gennaseret.

Is it a land bird that has lost its way? No,
But this is Mother Carey's chicken,
Harbinger of the storm.

O Mother Carey, green-toothed hag,
Mistress of the hurricane, your herds
The mighty choirs of singing whales, be lenient
To sailors and trawlermen, all who ply their way
Through dirty weather, over the hungry deep.

THE CORMORANT

A lone black crag stands offshore,
Lashed by the flying spray. Gorged from his fishing-foray
With long hooked beak and greenish glistering eye,
A cormorant, like a heraldic bird,
Spreads out dark wings, two tattered flags, to dry.

GREAT BLACK-BACKED GULLS

Said Cap'n Morgan to Cap'n Kidd:
"Remember the grand times, Cap'n, when
The Jolly Roger flapped on the tropic breeze,
And we were the terrors of the Spanish Main?"
And Cap'n Kidd replied: "Aye when our restless souls
Were steeped in human flesh and bone;
But now we range the seven seas, and fight
For galley scraps that men throw overboard."

126

Two black-backed gulls, that perched
On a half-sunken spar –
Their eyes were gleaming cold and through
The morning fog that crept upon the grey-green waves
Their wicked laughter sounded.

BLACK-HEADED GULLS FOLLOWING THE PLOUGH

No storm-weather sign this. For generations now
The gulls have learned to fly inland,
And feed at the plough, white beside dark rooks,
Their cries as harsh but shriller. But the sea –
The ship-delighting sea, the unharvested –
Glints only in a keen, cold, unkind eye.

THE CORIRA

Tripping in troops along the Italian shore,
Bold black and white with chestnut,
Curved bill, long legs, toes partly webbed –
Thus the corira, so said Aldrovandus
Four centuries ago. But since his day
No one has found plume or pinion
Or beak or claw of it.

Gryphon, phoenix and simurgh
Flap great mythical wings
Among the heavens of poetry. Plausible corira,
I'll grant you a small place within those realms
Who have this advantage – you were not fabulous
But merely non-existent.

THE HERON

An image remembered from boyhood – glimpsed
From a moving train: a pool,
Or else a brook which must have run perforce
Beside the tracks, and a heron standing,
Not in his grey stillness,
Watching the waters for his prey – but all in motion,
As he tries to get into his snaking gullet
A flapping, white-bellied, obstinate cuss of a fish.

THE CURLEW

Lord help all those lost up there tonight
From the treacherous bog, the precipice at their feet.
The mist lies low on the moors – and through it the calling,
The wild disconsolate calling. The cry of the whaup,
Men say it's unchancy.

THE SANDPIPER

Lively and clean from the hills, the waters of the beck
Tumble and ripple and swirl over the sands and gravel
Where a stone divides them. With pointed wings and tail, the
    sandpiper
Stands, bobbing and dipping where the sunlight
Flashes and glances over the eddies – then takes flight,
Uttering a pure, shrill, rapid call. Now in the whole valley
The crystal air holds, for a moment,
The liquid clarity of that small music.

THE LAPWING

The lapwing is a type of guile – that guile
Is elemental, sacrificial love.
She tumbles across the field, trailing
A simulated broken wing, to draw you off
From the hollow scrape or dried out cattle-footprint
Where lie the blotched and pear-shaped eggs, or else
The soft grey young ones crouch, obedient to her cries;
Or dive-bombs you, beating about your head
With loud, distracted and distracting screams –
Which superstition heard
As lost, rejected souls flying in the spring mists,
That mocked the Crucified upon the cross.

THE WATERHEN

The lily pads, and the lily's pale chalice
Float on the still pool. A dragon-fly
Darts above, a miniature
Futuristic aeroplane.
Demure, in black and grey,
With white beneath the tail, and that touch
Of scarlet on the brow and bill, the waterhen
Slips through the reeds, on delicate greenish feet.

THE OYSTERCATCHER

They say in the Highlands and the Western Isles –
This tale was made by men who knew
What being harried and pursued could mean – that Jesus,
Fleeing the malice of his enemies,
Went down to the wild shore, to find a cave to hide in.
But the sea-pies, flying
About the limpet-covered reef, with clear bright calls,
Took pity on him there, and in their scarlet beaks
Brought kelp and tangle to cover him completely.
The ruthless foe went by. And for that season
His cup of suffering passed.
                              Therefore the oystercatcher
Is of good fortune and well seen of men,
Running at the tide's edge
Upon the cockle and the mussel banks.

THE GREAT BUSTARD

On Salisbury Plain, by the great standing pillars
Of Avebury or Stonehenge – temples reared

To Sun, and changing Moon, and all
The glittering cohorts of the arching sky –

Among the scattered mounds, the Long and the Round Barrows,
Sepulchres of now-forgotten chieftains,

Noblest of running birds, the bustard once
Stalked before his wives, moustachioes bristling.

The bustards are all gone – they'll come no more:
Much too easy to shoot, much too good to eat.

On Salisbury Plain the military
Has taken over now, with tanks and guns,

Precision instruments of death – and human beings
Are much too easy to shoot.

THE PHEASANT

Cock-pheasant crows in the English wood,
Then struts into the clearing – magnificent,

129

With emerald casque, russet and white and black;
For he was made for Asiatic landscapes –
His lineage is of Colchis, land of the Golden Fleece,
Or further eastward where
Slant-eyed Chinese limned him,
With swift sure brush strokes, on their scrolls of silk.

THE HOUSE SPARROW

Citizen Philip Sparrow, who likes
To build and breed about our habitations –
   The little birds that fly through city smoke –

Prolific, adaptable, bold,
Untidy, cheerfully vocal –
   The little birds that quarrel in the eaves –

Grant him his right of freedom and, of your charity,
His dole of crumbs and kitchen scraps –
   The little birds that stand in the eye of God.

THE GREENFINCH

On a May morning,
In the greening time
I heard a greenfinch in a college garden
Set to his jargon in a leafy tree;
The long flat call-note, which will be repeated
Through all the hot and dusty days of summer,
Subsumed in a desultory twitter.
The lazy greenfinch, thick-set country cousin
Of the trim, suburban, caged canary –
Green, green, green he calls through the green leaves.

THE CHAFFINCH

There's apple-blossom now, for Spring
Has made a definite entrance. With smoke-blue cap,
White epaulettes, and breast a rusty pink,
The chaffinch hurries through his rapid song:
So may some dowdier Mimi Pinson
Be quick quick quick quick quick quick quick to hear,
And Coelebs not be long a bachelor.

130

GOLDFINCHES

The sweet-voiced, the elegant, the with gold banded,
The seven-coloured linnets – they fall
On purple thistle-heads, an eager charm
On heads of whitish down that drift to the wind:
Madonna's birds, that feed among the thorns.

THE YELLOWHAMMER

This small bird, yellow as the never-
Out-of-blossom gorse (when gorse
Is out of blossom, kissing's out of fashion.)
Reiterates his little
"A little bit of bread and no cheese!"
Through the long summer days,
When other birds are silent.

When I was younger, days were longer,
Summers were warmer, and always
The yellowhammer's song.

THE NIGHTJAR

Summer twilight – the sun has left the sky.
A faint glow lingers. Silvery Venus
Beams a message from its alien world.
On the tall grasses points of green fire,
Elf-eyes. The glow-worms hoist their lanterns,
Love-signals for their wandering knights. Listen, a voice –
Intermittent whirring, spinning, churning. Almost invisible,
A night-jar lies along the length of a bough,
Mottled, with frog-like gape. Then snaps his wings,
And flits along the glade, pursuing
The soft, furry moth, and the blundering dor.

THE SWALLOW

The swallow has returned, and we can say for sure
That spring is here, and summer will follow after.
All through our winter, around an African kraal
His steel-blue pinions flickered; now he's flown back
Thousands of miles, over the seas and mountains,
To build once more his nest in an English barn –
Hooray for the swallow and the weather he brings with him!

THE MISSEL-THRUSH

February brings its storms and rain,
Flooding the side-walks and the dirt-choked drain;
Into the north-west wind a missel-thrush
Shouts his defiance from a bare-twigged bush,
Sprinkling the air with notes that seem as bright
As crocus, or the yellow aconite.

THE BLACKBIRD

"Sooty-plumed blackbird with your golden bill,
Why is your song so sweet and clear and mellow?"
"I lubricate my voice with slugs and snails."
"And sometimes cherries, too?" "Well, do you grudge me those –
Who pay you richly with a summer tune?"

THE SPOTTED FLYCATCHER

He takes his stance on a gate-post
All the long day; makes quick
Excursions up into the air –
Snip! Snap! Snap! Snip! – snatching
The dancing flies out of their element.

THE YELLOW WAGTAIL

Red and white, the gentle Herefords wander
Through the lush water-meadow, plashy and green –
And gold with buttercup-gold, white with moon-daisies,
Lady-smocks, meadowsweet.
They go in a placid cowpat dream – with a flash
Of yellow at breast and throat, the wagtail
Darts in and out among them, and snaps
At the black and buzzing flies that are the beasts' annoy.

THE ROBIN

i

The north wind blows, a leaden
Sky lowers above;
Snow, snow everywhere
Over the grudging ground.

A solitary robin sings:
"Oh babes in the wood, poor babes in the wood –
Don't you remember the babes in the wood?"

ii

Cock-robin in spring, his breast
Is a flag of aggression, which says
"Get out! This front garden is mine,
These are my worms, my nesting-site, my hen-bird!
Get out! Be off! I'm warning you!" – his song
A splutter of defiant rage.

THE WREN

The pygmy troglodyte, with tail cocked,
Runs through his caves, which are
The twisted roots and debris of the copse;
Then gives a loud burst of sudden song,
And stops as suddenly. Like a clockwork bird
Someone has wound up.

THE STONECHAT

This little ruddy bird of stony places,
Too rough for the harrow,
Has the chink of pebbles inside his throat
To serve him for a song

THE WHEATEAR
for Shaun Traynor

The green wheat is in the ear; in Mediterranean vineyards
Vines have tiny flowers. On English down or wold
White Arse alights, a dweller in stony places:
"Excuse me, Brother Rabbit,
I need your spare accommodation."

THE REED WARBLER

And you, skilful basket maker,
Who harbour in the whispering sedge
And vocal reeds – the inconsequential
Loquacious prattle of waters
Has flowed into your song.

THE WOOD WARBLER, THE WILLOW WARBLER, AND THE CHIFF-CHAFF

I thought the leaves had come to life;
It was the leaf-green birds.

I thought the green leaves
Had found their singing voice – the high sweet trill,
The tinkling chimes dying away,
The soft *zip-zap* of earliest spring.

THE NIGHTINGALE

The inconspicuous nightingale
Is not so rare as you perhaps may think,

Being not at all averse from
Home Counties conurban shrubberies,

And sings at least as much
By day as through the night –

Such is the urgency, when May-time rules,
Of finding a mate, defending territory:

The common motives for his song, as for all birds.
So much for poets' fancies then?

And yet, and yet, and yet...
That clear high *terew*, that long crescendo,

The dark sob in the throat – these simulate
The tones of human passion,

Telling of tragic sorrows, Greek and unassuageable,
Or, as the Persians told, he sang

With wounded heart, pressing against a thorn,
In love with the opening rose, that silken-petalled jilt,

Who flings her perfume to the morning breeze –
With beauty that fades, beauty that is eternal.

THE BLACKCAP

The Southern folk can boast their nightingale,
  Which chirrups a high-class tune,
Just like Madame Adelina Patti,
  Under the summer moon;

But the Northern nightingale, he is the blackcap,
  Warbling the leaves between,
Where the oak and the ash and the bonny birch-tree
  Flourish and grow green.

O brave blackcap, O blithe blackcap
  You sing so rich and clear
In the oak and the ash and the bonny ivy
  At the season of the year.

THE TURTLE DOVE

One day, one day,
After the eagles of war have preyed,
When the flowers appear on the earth, and it is spring –
The time of the singing of birds – the turtle dove
(As when the first flood-waters fell away)

Will build her nest in the heart of the peaceful grove.

The New Dance of Death

BUTTERFLY HUNTER

A small boy is running over the downs
And through the woodland rides he goes. He barks his bony knees
Upon the mountainous rocks. He sweeps his net
Through the forests of the grasses, over
The swaying cities of the wild carrot,
Campanula-chiming spires. In his innocent glee,
He is unaware that the bright, feckless creatures he pursues
Are, each one, you or I,
Are those we loved – ah, when was that? – and lost
And inconsolably have mourned.

DEATH THE ICE-CREAM MAN

He tolls his bell in passing. In some districts
The tune he plays is "Red-nosed Rudolph" –
A red-nosed, fiery-eyed, and phantom reindeer,
Scudding over the tundra among the smoke of the yurts;
In others it's the Spring Song – impossible freshness,
Victorian, Mendelssohnian peace of mind;
But here it is "Lady Greensleeves" – she
Is the green-sleeved English earth, and she will gather
All of us into her bosom. The snowfruits,
The choc ices and the cornets he dispenses
Are cold as ultimate zero. He asks no payment –
Generous to pensioners.
But he has customers of every age;
As for the little ones – he's awfully fond of those.

DEATH AND PROFESSOR CHEIRON CHELIFER

You wander in the library, between the stacks, –
Or is it the turnings of the cemetery? –
Reading inscriptions on lichened headstones,
Or broken spines of books. The past eludes you still –
A beckoning fair one.

Me you confront at the last bend:
For you the future is my mask.
And now you are transmogrified
Into a footnote, or perhaps a gloss,
Caught in the very act
Of creeping into the text.

DEATH AND THE POLITICIAN

Right Honourable Sir, Right Honourable Madam –
Unfinished business. There is now a lobby
Which you must go into – total unanimity.
Forget about the opinion polls, forget
The jockeying for places. Nor will they help you now –
The stalwart ladies in their hats, the good dependable
Flat-capped party workers. The game of power,
Like every childhood game, must break off now –
When the bell tolls in the great clock tower, and the lights
Are going out in the Chamber as in Europe:
Who goes home? Who goes home?

DEATH AND THE TERRORIST

He thinks I am his servant. Hoist with his own petard,
He blows himself and half a hundred others
Out of time, and into emptiness. In the final blackness,
Every vision fades – Tír na n'Óg,
The Prophet's honeyed paradise of houris, and even
The beautiful federated cities of the future. Only, in that brief
    moment
The image of a naked, bleeding man,
Strung to two crossbars, crown of acacia thorns.

DEATH'S BEDSIDE MANNER

The glimmering square, the half-awakened bird-pipe –
Tennyson knew it all. Fragments of Tennyson
Rattle about in the skull. When the crab bites,
When the angina grips, when the stertorous breath –
Breath like a drowning man's, drowning in emptiness –
Gasps. Just out of earshot.
Beside the bed he stands, in his dark, formal suit,
With white and fine and surgeon's hands. He will administer
The ultimate, the infallible anodyne.

DEATH AND THE POET

"You know me. I'm the one you called
Soft names in muséd rhymes." " 'In muséd rhymes'
Means those I did not write, feeling them false.
But I do know you, you are the general thief,
Bitter to all men, but most of all to me,
Who lived by the bright shining images you stow
Into your swagbag. No soft names for you.
You grinning nothing!" "I am the silence
That's between the words, silence at the line's ending,
Without that, can be no prosody. And all my vast domain
Is compassed by a caesura. It is my hand arrests
The water that your name's inscribed upon.
We'll go together, seek Virgilian fields, where I'll transmute you
Into perdurable and laureate marble-stone."

DEATH AND THE LADY

You come late, but I knew you would come.
Arriving sooner, you had been less welcome –

Planting frost and fever in my bones,
Turning my blood to a strong poison;
Or else the door had opened, and you stalked in
With the face of Jack the Ripper.

Not much is left, but I give you all:
Never before to any of the others –
But first, your present. You will hand me
The small change of pain, and then
Costly, a black pearl, oblivion.

DEATH AND THE REVEREND SIMON SIMPLEX

"Remember Holbein's woodcut, where I call
Out of the field the good pastor in the midst of his sheep."
"But he was mitred and was croziered –
And I have never come by such accoutrements."
"The image stands, and you must come." "My hungry sheep,
With queasy appetites look up, and I suppose
Someone will feed them. I hope the wind that swells them
Was not my wind – rather the wind that rustles
Through all the Sunday papers, and whistles shrill
Out of the television screen. Well, anyway,
I should be glad to knock off now, glad of a long sleep:
Your hand in mine, my fellow-labourer."

DEATH THE DRY-CLEANER

Pass me your suit, your trousers, and your jacket,
Shirt, waistcoat, socks and everything,
Hair, skin, guts, bones, toenails. And now go home. Your naked
    essence
Walks the streets in all their chilly weather,
But unembarrassed. Though stripped down,
And bare, you now are indiscernible.
I do not know when you'll get back your things;
But rest assured you will do, good as new –
Yes – good as new, and better.

WINGS

"On steel-blue wings from Africa,
Over the desert drought, and the sea's tumbling sapphire,
The swallow will come back when spring returns;
But for me," said Youth, "there's no returning."

"I come on the nightingale's brown wings,"
Said Love, "to perch in the moonlit glade,
Singing my song, singing my sweet, sweet prick-song,
My breast against a thorn, impaled
Upon the eternal, never thornless rose."

"Hawk-winged I come," so said the cuckoo, Jealousy,
"To foist my monstrous and insatiate offspring
In that fragile cradle, where
Nurture their naked bantlings Eros and Psyche –
Papageno, Papagena."

"Out of the twilight, out of the darkness, sometimes
A prodigy at noonday, I swoop down
With muffled plumes, and with extended talons:
I come on the owlet's wings," said Azrael.

The Great Yahoo Revolution

After Gulliver had left the island
They still remembered him. While he had been among them
They had rather disliked him. They thought him stuck-up and
    prissy,
With his mincing ways, his patent contempt for them,
His cringing subservience to their masters –
Almost, you would say,
A houyhnhnm in a yahoo's hide. But afterwards
His image began to change in their folk-memory,
Presenting a possible yahoo perfectibility –
Fragrantly un-hirsute, and non-nude,
And full of mysterious skills and expertise:
Witness his ticking watch that talked to him,
Witness his pocket compass,
And, above all, his pistols.

Poets arose,
Singing of the world's great age which begins anew,
As they crouched around their fires of cattle-dung,
And scrambled for the orts the houyhnhnms allotted them.
Bards twanged on gut-string stretched across dried gourds,
Fluted on hollow bones, foretold

How soon a scarlet dawn should come,
When the yahoo race should rise to gain its freedom
And all be Gullivers.

And so, surprisingly, that day did come:
The yahoos revolted – armed with nothing more
But sharpened sticks and flaked flint-stones,
And primitive ploughshares, they fought against
The flailing hoofs and crunching teeth of their masters.

Leaders now appeared as if from nowhere;
Names to be honoured through the generations:
The noble Hoo-ha, the heroic Uggie,
And that great feminine apostle of liberation,
Stinkastinkah, the carrotty-haired one.
The houyhnhnms' leaders were slaughtered and roasted –
Some of them roasted alive. There were forty days
Of feasting on horse-steaks, on horse-liver, on horse-tripes,
And guzzling on the superior quality oats
The houyhnhnms always reserved for their own use –
All this washed down with the heady drink
Those slaves themselves had devised,
Brewed from the wild bee-honey, and forest fruits,
Which the houyhnhnms contemned, but allowed them to use,
Because it had kept them stupid.

But after that things settled down:
There was convened a great popular assembly,
Which all of them attended,
In spite of bloated stomachs and sore heads.
They hammered out laws, and a constitution.
A republic was proclaimed, and Stinkastinkah
Became first president. Later on
Her office was confirmed for life. But Uggie and Hoo-ha
Dissented, and retired with all their followers,
To sulk upon the northern and the southern promontories,
Which seemed sterile. But the central plain
(And here it was that Stinkastinkah's writ ran
And her successors in the female line)
Was rich in pasturage and had abundant corn-land.

The surviving houyhnhnms were reduced to servitude,
Set to the plough, to labour in the quarries,
Hauling great blocks of stone for buildings,

Or in the depths of the earth, in the newly discovered mines,
Or, with tight bearing-rein and under the lash,
They pulled the coaches of the yahoo notables.

The high and noble classic houyhnhnm language
Degenerated into a series of inarticulate
Neighings and whinnyings. But mostly these poor beasts were
    silent,
Pensively nodding as they did their tasks,
Or dreaming in their draughty stalls at night.
What did they dream of? They had always believed
In a Supreme Being, exalted, passionless and abstract,
But now that myth assumed a different form:
He was a great winged stallion, colour of starlight,
Up in the pastures of the cumulus clouds.
The thunder was the rattling of His hoof beats;
His eyes flashed lightning, and the snorting tempest
His angry breath. One day He'd descend to earth,
A Saviour God, and lead the houyhnhnm nation
Over the rainbow bridge into celestial paddocks.

The Yahoo state prospered. They achieved remarkable progress.
The Dutch voyager, Adrianus Vanderflick,
Who touched there in the seventeen nineties,
Found a people, simple and pastoral,
Skilled in equestrian matters, but already
Exhibiting signs of technological development.

The promontories which
The followers of Uggie and Hoo-ha occupied,
Had rich deposits – coal and iron, nitre,
Petroleum and uranium ore,
And somehow they discovered how to use these,
Especially when the civil wars began
Between the Uggites and the Stinkastinkists
(The Hoo-ha party tactically changing sides,
Holding the balance). Since Vanderflick's time
Few have reached that island, but there are rumours in our own
    century
Of a barren, slightly radioactive rock,
Strewn with the skeletons of horses,
And other bones, reputed to be human.

Moving to Winter

As I move, through autumn to winter, my life's house
Is Edmund Waller's cottage of the soul.
How chill, how pure, eternity shines through the chinks!
Yet, while my fire still burns, I'll proffer
Scraps of toasted cheese to the crickets –
My long-legged, whiskery poems, that chirp in the crannies,
Or hop about on the flagstones. And there'll be other visitants –
    an incognito
Angel or so, all my accustomed ghosts,
And, twirling his forked tail, pedunculate-eyed,
With sharp, nine-inch proboscis for a nose,
Not all malignant, the odd domestic bogle.

On the Demolition of the Odeon Cinema
Westbourne Grove

Never one for the flicks, I did not frequent the place:
Though I recall the *Voyage of the Argonauts*,
And a second feature – some twaddle about
A daughter of King Arthur, otherwise unrecorded
By history or tradition. Now, each day,
I pass it, and I hear the brutal noise
Of demolition: clatter of falling masonry,
Machines that seem to grit and grind their teeth,
And munch in gluttony of destruction.

Its soft innards, I guess, are gone already:
The screen, the lighting, the plush seats; the ghosts likewise –
Shadows of shadows, phantoms of phantoms,
The love goddesses, the butcher boy heroes,
The squawking cartoon-animals.

This odeon – I should regret it? –
In which no ode has ever been recited.
Yet there's a pang – for I've lived long enough
To know that every house of dreams
Must be torn down at last.

142

Martinmas

Only half a cloak of warmth and sunlight –
Gold thread woven in the mist – the month flings down
Upon our northern world. Pinched by the Scorpion's claws,
Pierced by the Archer's icy shafts, the earth,
Shivering, turns towards the solstice.

I think how El Greco saw St Martin –
A young hidalgo of his own century:
With elegant, practised hand he unsheathes
His fine Toledo blade, and slits
The sumptuous mantle – velvet, silken,
Gold embroidery thread – to cast it down
(And yet with courtesy) a gift to the poor shivering man who
    crouches
Close to his horse's hooves –

And then rides on, maybe to join a party.
Where his companions chaff him: "Look at Señor Half-cloak!"
"Is this the latest winter fashion, do you think?"

How cold, how keen, the wind of the spirit blows
Through all the crannies of the chicken-coops
That we would hide in. Martin,
The cock that crowed for Peter crows for you.

As for the beggar, half a cloak for him
Was a lot better than no cloak at all;
And twisted round his starved and scabby body
It kept the life in him, a season and a season –
Who, in the end, lay dead in a ditch, perhaps, and never knew
In him the naked Christ was clothed – not till he woke
In that green parkland where it's always spring,
And always Easter morning.

Holy Innocents' Day

After inexplicable music in the sky,
The shepherds' pipe and drum, and Mary's song,
In the darkened villages, the screams:
The soldiery have come –
Rachel is weeping for her children.

143

Never a Christmas can go by, but you
Must think of children Famine crams
Into her bread-basket, of those red War
Has roasted, suffocated, disembowelled, and those
Whose violated bodies lie on building sites,
Or else in dustbins like discarded dolls;
And think of Gilles de Retz
Who built a chapel for the Holy Innocents.

Four Dragons

St George rides down the vale to Uffington,
White horsed. There are four dragons
He must encounter now.

The first dragon was of the earth.
Out of its ripped-up belly tumbled
Jewelled goblets, golden torques, and helmets,
Swords of Wayland's workmanship.
The men of former times had hidden them.

The second dragon was of the air.
The great black cumulo-nimbus
Burst. The rains streamed down.
Clad in the greenness of the growing corn
Came forth the young spring bride out of the furrow.

The third dragon was of the water.
The river rose. Redeemed from human sacrifice,
In all her finery, the king's daughter
Danced in triumph. Silver anklets
Tinkled upon her feet.

The fourth dragon was of the fire.
Slowly and cruelly the flames licked upwards,
Reaching for the hand – the martyr's hand
That had so contumaciously torn down
Caesar's persecuting edict.